Psalms Turned Inward:

A Woman talks with her God

Adrienne Keller

Copyright © 2018 Adrienne Keller

All rights reserved.

ISBN: 978-1727355796

DEDICATION

For Woody, beloved husband & garden muse

INTRODUCTION

Several years ago, as I read the psalms, I realized that *my* worst enemies were internal, not external. Demons, attackers, agnostics, atheists, fighters and haters — all inside me. So I began to rewrite the psalms to reflect that. I began to do what I have called internalizing, personalizing the psalms – speaking to God about myself and speaking to God about Herself. Eventually, I decided to record my efforts in a simple blog, through WordPress, at ***vabutsy.com***. A couple of years later, I expanded the blog to include some other things I write.

As I journeyed through the psalms and made them my own, I found myself more and more aware of the feminine, the womanly, the motherly in God. And so I have chosen words for God, including pronouns, that are feminine, or at least gender neutral (like sovereign rather than king). The proverbial Lady Wisdom revealed herself to me through the psalms. In my psalm poems you will find me referring to God as Lady Wisdom or Wisdom Woman.

Similarly God revealed my worst foes to be largely captured in what I now call my terrible Ds: depression, doubt, discouragement, darkness, distractions, dis-ease, death. You will find me using that phrase, "my terrible Ds", repeatedly. My version of Psalm 109 recounts how these wound me.

My psalm poems are based upon and with quotes mainly from the NIV and NSRV-Catholic Edition. Other translations and books on the psalms that have influenced me are listed in the Bibliography at the end. (Of course I have a Bibliography, because I am still an academic, even in retirement).

Adrienne Keller
November 2018
Charlottesville, Virginia

Psalm 1

Blessed can I be
If I avoid walking in anger
Standing around feeling sorry for myself
Sitting smugly judging others
Instead may I focus on the good
And turn my mind always to God's positive
Then my life will take shape like a fruitful tree
Watered by fresh flowing streams
("A tree that talks to God all day
And lifts her leafy arms to pray")
I will not wither and shrivel into the negative
I will feel prosperous, nourished and nourishing
The alternative is not at all attractive
My life becomes like dead leaves
Blown every which way by discouraging thoughts
My tree will be bowed down, broken and uprooted
I will be unable to enjoy goodness and good people
The good choice supports light and life
The other choice brings darkness and a living death. Amen

Psalm 2

I seem to have warring nations inside me
Different people plotting, striving, in vain
Too often, those with the upper hand take their stand against peace
Against Sovereign Lady Wisdom
Then I see religion only as chains of duties
Fetters of narrow-mindedness
And yet I come back, again and again
To the glory and the light of the One in heaven
The One who scoffs at my naysayers
The One who rebukes my depression
In God's glory, gloom cannot stay
Up and up God takes my vision
To God's holy Ruler on high
With relief, with gratitude I can say
That I belong to God
That I get to claim God's protection
God promises me a wonderful inheritance
The ability to conquer those warring nations inside me
So I remind myself to be wise
To serve the Ruler of light and rejoice
To kiss the Daughter of peace
And turn away from depression and anxiety
Blessed are all who take refuge in Lady Wisdom. Amen

Psalm 3

O God, how many are my discouraging thoughts
How often they rise up against my peace
Many times I say to myself
"It's hopeless. There is no God to deliver me."
But here is what I want to believe
That You are a shield around me
That You bestow glory on me and lift up my life.
So to You I turn and cry aloud in my mind
Praying You will answer me from heights of holy hope
When I lie down and sleep
When I wake again, sustain me, please
Remind me that I need not fear
The tens of thousands of discouraging thoughts
Ready to defeat me on every side, in every effort
Rise, Rise up above those pitfalls, oh my soul
Rise up to goodness and light
Deliver me, O my God
From the gaping mouths and sharp teeth
Of depression and despair,
From dark images and defensiveness
The God of light brings deliverance
May your blessing be on me as one of your people. Amen

Psalm 4

Please answer me when I call to You
O my righteous God
Relieve my distress
Have mercy and hear my prayer
Otherwise, on my own, I turn glory into shame
I delude myself and seek false gods
I need to remember that God has set apart the godly for goodness
I need to remember that God will hear me when I call
I truly do not want anger and envy to rule my life
When I lie in bed each night and search my heart
I want to find peace and silence
I want to know that I have made good choices
That I have trusted in God
With many others, I ask "Who can show us any good?"
I can find the answer in the light of Your shining face, O God
Looking back on my life
I realize that You have filled my heart with greater joy
Than any riches or benefits, honors or achievements
When I remember this, I can lie down and sleep in peace
Knowing that in You alone, O God, I dwell in safety and goodness. Amen

Psalm 5

Hear my words and my sighs, O God
Hear my cry for help, my Sovereign Lady Wisdom
For I don't know where else to turn but to You
In the morning, every morning,
I will lay my needs before You
And then wait with hope
Knowing that You do not promote wrong-headedness
You destroy lies, envy and deceit
Only by Your great mercy will I be able to come into Your house
And bow down to You
Only if You lead me in Your righteousness
Away from the wrongness that is the enemy I fear
Only if You make straight Your way for me
Away from the crooked wrong way
Where I can't trust my own thoughts or feelings
Away from the treacherous sinkholes of depression and self-disgust
Deceit and envy
I need Your help, O God, to recognize them, declare them unworthy
Banish them!
They have no place in righteousness
Love and gratitude, generosity and kindness, courage and laughter
Faithfulness and light:
Let these have Your protection and help
Be my refuge and gladness
I want to sing with joy
Protect me
Help me to love goodness and rejoice in righteousness
For surely, O God, You bless righteousness
You surround goodness with Your shield. Amen

Psalm 6

O God, when I forget You, here is what happens to me
I feel deserted, disciplined
I can't see any light; my world grows dim and gray
Not just my spirit but even my body starts to fall apart
My thoughts come back again and again
To feeling sorry for myself
I know this but can't save myself
I need you, God, to deliver me
Because Your steadfast love and light never fails, never dims
But I can't remember You when I am caught
In the dark grave of depression and despair
I can't see You; I can't lift myself out
I just lie there, moaning and groaning
Wearing myself out with depressing thoughts
Now, while I can, I call out to You
Please, please, God, protect me from these very real enemies
See my weakness, hear my cry for help, accept my prayer
Let my darkness vanish in Your light. Amen

Psalm 7

God, my God, I take refuge in you
Asking You, begging You
To save me from the darkness that pursues me
Please don't let it destroy my peace
Don't let me tear my own life apart
Don't let me feel sorry for myself
As if there is no one who can help me
God, my God, when I forget You
When my thoughts go only downward
Then I have no peace of mind; I rob myself of happiness
I let all the dark and negative overtake me
I live in shadow; I sleep in dust
God, my God, arise in my mind and lift me up
Up and up lift my thoughts
Away from my own darkness and doubt
Away from depression and despair
Awake in my mind, in my life, my God
Awake and bring truth and goodness
Gather my thoughts and feelings around You
Rule over them from on high; judge them
Pick and choose those that are worthy
Those that will help me live life well
Those that are true and good, like You Yourself
O my good and true God
My Creator who knows my mind and heart
You can bring an end to the violence I do myself
You can make my goodness strong
You can be ruler of my mind and heart
You can keep me hopeful, loving, faithful
I need to remember that I can depend on God
God is powerful, never negative, never defeated by darkness
God's bright weapons are aflame
They burn through my darkness
When I am filled with doubt, despair, gloom and doom,
When I fall into the hole I have dug for myself,

When the violence I do to myself begins to tear me down
Then, then to God, to my Sovereign God Lady Wisdom
I need to turn my thoughts and feelings
To brightness and power, to hope and love
Up, up and up, to light, to thankfulness
To my powerful God
I need to sing praises to God Most High. Amen

Psalm 8

O God, my God,
Let Your name be majestic in all my life
May Your glory always shine brightly above all else in my life
When I was young
I learned to sing Your praise
I learned You were stronger than any worries or wrongness
Now, I look to this universe that is Your work
The moon, the stars and everything around us
To remind myself of Your power and sovereignty
You are responsible for everything and everyone
Yet You pay attention to me individually
You love me
You want me to live well
With glory and honor
You give me the ability to rule my life
To control the beasties and burdens
That threaten me
O God, my God
How majestic is Your name in all my life. Amen

Psalm 9

I want to praise you, God, with all my heart
I want to tell of all Your wonders
Rejoicing in You, singing praises to Your name, O Most High
Will make me happy and content
Then there will be no place for my worst thoughts and fears
They will perish before You
For You lift up and light up my mind and heart
You are a true judge of my thoughts and feelings
You have the right and the power
To keep me whole, keep me true
Keep me safe from the enemies within
The weeds in my mind that invade my peace
Envy, suspicion, depression, alienation
You can blot them out forever
You can uproot them
So that I forget the darkness and live in the light
For myself, I want God to reign forever
To be my judge and my gardener
To govern my unruly heart
To be my refuge when I feel oppressed
My stronghold when I am troubled
If I can only remember to call on You, God
If I can only remember
That You have never forsaken those who seek You
Then I can sing praises with a light heart
Sing praises to my Sovereign enthroned in my heart
Then I can silence all my fears with Your name
Because You do not ever forget me as I sometimes forget You
You never ignore my cries for help
But You can see what has happened to me
Too often, I let darkness rule in my life
Have mercy and lift me up out of my darkness that strangles hope
Lift me up so I can praise You
And rejoice in Your power, in my salvation
Lift me up out of the pit I dig for myself

Out of the weeds of doubt that entangle me
You, You are known by Your justice and truth
I am in danger of being ensnared by my own worst tendencies
Of falling again into the pit of depression
Of forgetting God
So all I can do is depend on Your enduring faithfulness
You do not forget me
You remain my hope
Arise, God, arise in my mind
Don't let the dark and worldly parts of me win
Rule my mind and my heart
Weed the garden of my soul
Flood it with Your light
Banish my darkness – it is nothing compared to You. Amen

Psalm 10

Why, O God, do I keep You at a distance
Just when I need You most
In my arrogance, I turn to my weakest parts
I catch myself up in my own twisted thoughts
I pay attention to all the wrong feelings
I dwell on the lowest of my desires
And forget You
Forget to seek You
In all my thoughts, I make no room for You
I puff myself up, I sneer at those I do not like
I forget Your steadfast love and forgiveness
Briefly, briefly, I feel so full of myself
So pleased with my own successes
I boast to myself of my insight
I win arguments and put down those I am angry with
All in my own mind
Instead of remembering "God is here"
I keep coming back and back to my anger, my hurt pride
My thoughts ambush my peace, murder my quiet
Drag my contentment through the mud of my discontent
Until I collapse under my own unkind thoughts

Then I am likely to decide that God has forgotten me
When really I have forgotten God
So rise up in my mind, please, O God
Help my helplessness
Restore my peace
Keep me from being my worst
You do see my trouble and grief
You can take it in hand
I commit myself to You
You are the helper of the helpless
Break through my anger and discontent
God is Sovereign for ever and ever
Darkness disappears in God's light
You hear, O God, my desire when I am afflicted

By my own weaknesses and failings
You encourage my goodness, my strength
You listen to my cry for help
You defend me against my self-destruction
I have to believe that You can free me
From the terror of my own anger. Amen

Psalm 11

In God I take refuge
Except, of course, for the parts of me that say
"There is no God, you're on your own
Look how long you have struggled to 'be good'
Have you ever managed?
Don't the same ungenerous thoughts keep coming back and back?
Don't you struggle still and always with envy and discouragement?"
Time and again the thoughts that I hate take aim
To kill my peace of mind
Time and again my security is shaken to the foundations
Time and again I wonder what I can do to restore my tranquility
That's when I have to remember:
God is on the heavenly throne
In the throne room of my interior castle
God can help me
God knows when I am in trouble of my own making
God loves me, God loves me, God loves me
My own failings can't defeat me
Because God defeats them
With righteousness and steadfast love for me
For God is righteous and God loves justice
And God loves me – and so we can meet face to face
Though God is almighty
And I am just me.
So I can take refuge in God. Amen

Psalm 12

Help me, God, I am too often unfaithful
Filled with doubt
Lying to myself
Flattering myself
Deceiving myself
Banish my lies
Silence my boasting
Help me to remember
That it is not by my worthiness that I am saved
But by Your grace
I trust You to arise in my mind and heart
I trust You to protect me from my own doubts
In You I find silver truth
In You I find golden strength
In You I find sweet safety
The answer to my neediness
The protection of my righteousness
So that I will not ever honor what is vile and useless
But will rest secure in Your protection forever. Amen

Psalm 13

I come to You, God, having failed yet again
Failed in loving
Will this be my whole life?
Can I never love in imitation of Your steadfast love?
How long must I wrestle with my thoughts
And every day have sorrow in my heart?
How long will anger and hurt triumph over me?
Look on me and help, O God
Be Ruler of my life
Lighten my heart or this deathly heaviness will persist
I will be lost in my own dark thoughts
Spiraling ever down into resentment and judgment
Impatience and anger

BUT, writes the psalmist – the but that I want so much to live
I trust in Your steadfast love
(So very different than my temperamental likes and pouts)
My heart rejoices in Your salvation
(So save me already from failing to live Your steadfast love)
Save me so that, with the psalmist I can say, shout, sing, live
So others can see that
I sing to God, of God, with God, by God
For God has been good to me. Amen

Psalm 14

When I am foolish, my heart tells me
"There is no God"
All I see is corruption, vileness
My world becomes a dreary and wicked place
I imagine God looking down on us
Wanting us to seek Her
I imagine God turning away in disgust
I imagine no God, I imagine nothingness
I turn away, feeling that I am as corrupt, as vile,
As lacking in goodness
As everyone and everything else
I forget, time and again
I fail to learn, I fail to remember
I stop calling on God
I let myself be overwhelmed by dread
But my forgetfulness, my fears
Cannot change the reality of God
God remains present, with all that is good and righteous
God remains the refuge of my impoverished understanding
My salvation comes from the usual place
From God—God who alone restores me. Amen

Psalm 15

God, when am I within your holy shelter
Lifted high by Your grace and righteousness?
When my walk is blameless
When I do what is right
When I speak the truth from my heart
When my tongue utters no slander
When I do no wrong to a neighbor
When I cast no slurs on others
When I don't give in to my worst tendencies
But live a life that pleases You
When I keep a promise even when it hurts
When I don't let go of my beliefs
When I give to the poor
When I support the innocent
And I believe I can live like this
With Your grace. Amen

Psalm 16

Guard my mind and heart, O God,
To You I turn seeking a peaceful spirit
Here's what I have come to know:
I am better, happier when I am Yours
When I forget You, my inner world descends into turmoil
Your saints – living and dead – help me to remember You
They show me the joy of living with You
On my own, I only increase my sorrow and confusion
When I turn away, when I start doubting, stop praying
And let my worldly concerns rule my life
Keep me in prayer, please
Keep me from letting preoccupations and worries,
Hurt and heaviness rule my mind and heart
Help me to remember that You are God
You love me; in You I have security and peace
With You I find pleasure and peace, delight and light

I want to live my life praising You, not doubting You
I want to know Your wisdom, Your peace each night
I want to set You always before me
Letting Your light banish my darkness
Mind, heart and body are well with You
You will not abandon me to my dark despair
You will not let me rot in anger and worry
In You I find my way to life and light, to energy and joy
Forever. Amen

Psalm 17

Hear, O God, my desperate plea
Listen to my crying
Pay attention to my prayer (please)
I do my best to be truthful with You
So that my life may flow from You
Reflecting Your goodness
I want to live so that when You probe my mind and heart
You will find them bright with Your own light
When I speak, my words will be kind and true
But You know me
I do try, but I often fail
I try to walk in Your grace and light
But still I stumble into darkness
Letting all of the unhelpful negatives block my walk with You
So I call on You, O God, trusting that You will answer me
I ask again
Listen to my crying
Pay attention to my prayer (please)
Show me the wonder of Your steadfast love
Lift me up
Turn me to Your bright face
Keep me as the apple of Your eye
Let me hide, not in the shadows of my own making
But in the shadow of Your bright wings
Let me hide in Your shadow
From the dark feelings that trouble me
From the thoughts that kill my joy
Keep my heart soft
Let me live in Your humility
Not in my own arrogant pride
I am so afraid—afraid of my own worst tendencies
My darkness, my arrogance, my despair, my envy
I try to walk with You
But they track me down, surround me
Trip me up, throw me down

They will devour my happiness, my abilities, my peace
Rise up in my mind and heart, O God
Rise up in my life
Let Your peace and goodness rise up
And bring down my darkness and troubles
Cut through my doubts and daydreams
O God, save me from living a life in darkness
Save me from focusing only on this world
In You I can find what I seek, what I need
In You my hungering soul can be filled
In You my poor struggling heart can find a wealth of peace
And I will see Your face reflected in all this world
I will say, always, "God is here"
And I will awake with hope, not dread. Amen

Psalm 18

I love you, O God, my strength.
God is my strong foundation, my security, my savior
God is my refuge from despair
My shield of hope
My salvation call and my stronghold against doubt
I call upon God, God who is worthy of my praise and adoration
I call upon God because only She can save me
From those terrible Ds
Death, destruction, despair, doubt, depression, distractions
Attack me
Enclose me
Drown me
Entangle me
Trap me
In my distress, I called upon God
To my God, to Sovereign Lady Wisdom, I cried for help
I don't know, can't understand where God is
It is enough that I know God heard me
My cry for help found Her and She heard me
Oh my, how the psalmist does picture God's might for me
I feel my world reeling and rocking
The foundations of my pride and doubt trembling and quaking
Is She angry with me? Or just coming in power to save me?
Stronger than the heavens
Swifter than the wings of the wind
More powerful than the deepest darkness
Bright fire, saving thunder
Arrows of faith piercing my heart
Lightning striking through my disbelief
The waters of my forlorn tears dry up
The universe is revealed as God's creation
Formed by Her breath
Oh, I agree with the psalmist
God rescued me, rescues me
Not once, but again and again
She lifts me up from depression
She supports me in my faith

She delivers me from doubt
And She delights in me, loves me, cherishes me
But NOT, oh not, because of my righteousness
It is not my hands that are clean
For I have not kept the ways of God
I have departed, again and again, from God
So often have I failed to love others
To see God in others
I am not blameless, I have not kept myself from guilt
And yet, and yet, oh wonders of wonders
God has rescued me because of Her own righteousness
Out of Her own love
This is love, not that I love God, but that She first loved me
Though I was lost in my terrible Ds.

O God, when I am loyal to You, I feel Your loyalty
When I feel good, I feel Your goodness
When I forget You, I think You forget me
When I am lost and unhappy, I think You perverse and fickle
As if I created You, as if I control You
But You are constant, You are true
You are enduring faithfulness and steadfast love
You are a God of contradictions
Delivering the humble, humbling the proud
The light of faith lights up my darkness
By You, with You, I defeat my terrible Ds
I leap over my wall of doubt and distractions

Lady Wisdom's way is perfect
Her promises – for me – are true
She is my mother hen protector
Who is Lady Wisdom except YHWH?
Who is my strong foundation except God?
God who strengthens my faith
Lady Wisdom who makes my way safe
She supports me as I walk through life's challenges
Faith in Her becomes my highest high
In Her I find my surest defeat of my terrible Ds

In Her I find my strongest support
Like a shield, Her love protects me
Like a wide ledge, Her help eases my way
With Her help, I chase away my terrible Ds
"I struck them down, so that they were not able to rise
They fell under my feet"
For God strengthens me and redeems me
God takes care of my enemies, those terrible Ds
That would destroy me
They try, oh they still try, time and again
They tell me they are supreme in my life
But God does not make them supreme
No, She rescues me, She gives me victory
So I can beat my doubt into dust
Trample my depression and rise above it
She delivered me from distractions
She gave me charge over my own life
Supporting me through troubles unknown
Through all of my trials, all of my troubles
Through all the possibilities of my life
God, my Sovereign God, supports me
And gives me victory
(Even when it does no look or feel like victory)
God lives! Blessed be my strong foundation
Exalted be the God of my salvation
God, Sovereign Lady Wisdom, who gives me peace
Who subdues my angers and my discouragement
Who delivers me from my terrible Ds
Exalted God who delivers me from my own violence
For this, O God, I extol you in my whole life
For this, O God, and so much more, I sing praises to Your name
Great triumphs She gives to me
And shows me Her steadfast love
Through all the ages of my life. Amen

Psalm 19

The heavens declare the glory of God
The skies proclaim the work of God's hands
Day after day they shout it out; night after day they show me
Without words, beyond hearing, they speak to my heart
They proclaim God's glory to all the earth, to the ends of the world
Just as example consider the sun:
Its beauty, its power, its steadiness, its daily journey
How its energy impregnates the earth
Powerful Creator
Let Your energy penetrate me so that I remember this:
Your way is perfect, reviving my soul
Your way is trustworthy, making me wise
Your way is right, bringing me joy
Your way is bright, lighting my life
You way is pure, giving me lasting peace
Your way is sure and altogether righteous
Your way is the golden way, better than gold
Your way is the honeyed way, better than honey
Like the sun warms the earth
Your way warms me and brings me true reward
You know I am often blind to my own failings
You know how negative thoughts, depressed feelings can ambush me
Forgive me and help me; don't let darkness rule over me
Let my thoughts, words and deeds reflect Your light
O God, my strong foundation and redeemer. Amen

Psalm 20

Oh dear God, answer me when I am in distress
Can the name of the God of that great cloud of witnesses,
Those thousands of years of believers, really protect me?
God of peace, help me
God of strength, support me
Remember me, remember my prayers
Remember the times I offered You my contrite heart
Give me good and holy desires
Let my worthy plans succeed
Give me faith and hope, courage and conviction
Confidence and joy, victory over my warring emotions
Let me know this, remember this:
That You give victory to those who turn to You
You answer prayers
You lend me Your own power
Sometimes I trust in yoga, sometimes in psychology
Sometimes in others, sometimes in myself
But when I trust in You, when I trust in You
Ah, then I fall to my knees to worship You
Yet stand firm against my own weaknesses
So give me a royal victory
Answer me when I remember to call on You
(Please and thank You). Amen

Psalm 21

O God, I am so thankful for Your strength, for Your help
With You I can know the joy of victory over darkness
I come to You not just asking that You grant the desires of my heart
But that You help me to have worthwhile desires
I need help to discern true blessings, to appreciate true goodness
So that my life may be crowned with the golden crown of Your peace
Only in You can I find life everlasting
Only in You can I know greatness
Only in You can I see splendor and majesty
Only You can grant eternal blessings
Only in Your presence can I sustain joy
So here's my prayer, my only prayer or at least my main prayer
Help me to remember that
Help me to trust in You
Help me to remember that in Your steadfast love
I can find an end to my questioning and doubting and troubles
Turning to You, I can overcome my inner struggles
You can seize them, squeeze them into kindling
Swallow them up in the furnace of Your bright love and power
Burn them forever from my immortal soul
I may have to struggle with them while I live here
But You will ensure that they do not follow me into eternity
Your weapons of steadfast love and peace will pierce them
I exalt in Your strength, I praise Your might, I sing of You. Amen

Psalm 22

(OK, this feels just a bit presumptuous; this to me is the psalm of the cross and even though I don't always accept the Gospel version as necessarily reality, it still feels like something I should not mess with)

My God, my God, I feel like You have forsaken me
(Even though I may deserve to be forsaken
That has never been Your way)
You seem to be so far from saving me
So far from my groaning and moaning
I feel like I cry out to You day and night, but get no answer
Aren't You the holy one, the eternal one, God almighty of Israel
Yada yada yada
Wasn't I taught that all of those great cloud of witnesses
Trusted You and were not disappointed
What about me? What am I, a worm?
You know what it feels like to be paranoid?
To worry that everyone is looking down on you
Secretly insulting you, shaking their heads
Saying it's too bad, what a waste, she had such promise
God help her since about all she has left is God
OK, so maybe all I ever had was You
That's certainly what I was taught
Didn't really have to be taught it – I learned it in the womb
So come on, don't give up on me
I feel threatened, threatened by my own bull-headedness
Threatened by the beasts of my own darkness
The ones that chew up my confidence and spit it out in little pieces
The ones that make me feel powerless, like a scarecrow
With all the stuffing gone, a poor limp thing that crows nest on
I feel like death, ready to be eaten by dogs, beaten by life
Mourned over, gloated over, ignored, naked

So I guess I'm counting on You, God, to be my strength
To come quickly to help me
To save me from my own dark and fearsome terrors
From my own depression and despair
From the ravaging beasts of my self-doubts and delusions
The psalmist promises to declare Your name, to praise You
I have to admit that I often forget to do that
"Praise God, honor God, revere God," instructs the psalmist
I promise to try but You know that even to do that I need You
So don't hide Your face from me
Please answer my cries for help
Then let me use Your blessings to help other
Not just to praise You to others, with others
But to truly help those in need; help me to do my part
All my life, let me know You and turn to You
Let me bow down before You, my Creator God
Let me know that what I do, I do only through You
What I have, I have only through You
Who I am, I am only through You
Let my life speak to my children and grandchildren
My family and friends
Let my life show Your greatness not my fears
Let my life show Your strength not my weakness
Let my life show Your righteousness not my failings
Let my life show that You have done what needed to be done. Amen

Psalm 23

The Word of God promises me that if I let God be my guide
She will take care of me, give me peace and quiet
Make sure that my thoughts and actions are righteous
So that even when I am overwhelmed by deathly anger
By stinking depression, by sinking doubts
I will be OK
God will stay with me, defend me, comfort me
Better than that
God will let me feel like I am feasting at a banquet
Relaxing untouched by the hungering dark
Overflowing with everything good and true
If only, if only, if only I could live like that always
Then surely I would not have to struggle so
Just to feel good, just to hold others in thoughts of mercy
Rather than thoughts of anger and disappointment
If only I could let God be my guide forever. Amen

(A pause here because although I can read and write these words
Although I feel that these psalms are true
Tonight is one of my times of darkness
When all I really feel about myself is unworthy
I feel alone and unloved, and what is worse,
I feel that it is right and just that I am alone and unloved
I feel this fate to be no more or less than what I have brought on myself
I am drowning in pity here
And I hate it
Come on, God, give a little, can't You?
A little bit of rescuing is in order here & would be much appreciated.)

Psalm 24

Everything and everyone belongs to God
Because God created everything
God created everyone to share in divine glory
And that includes me
I belong to God
God wants me to be content, to live in truth
To recognize truth and respond to it
In truth, God blesses and saves me
Even from myself
If I – like that great cloud of witnesses
Turn to the bright light of God's face
Away from the darkness of my fears and doubts.
So let me lift up my thoughts, lift up my feelings, lift up my actions
Each day
Lift them up to my sovereign God
Who is this God of glory, this Wisdom Woman?
God strong and mighty
Strong enough, mighty enough to conquer my troubles
So let me lift up my thoughts, lift up my feelings, lift up my actions
Each day
Lift them up to my sovereign God
Who is this God of glory, this Wisdom Woman?
None other than the true God, the mightiest God, the only God
Ruler of glory, Bringer of light, Conqueror of fears. Amen

Psalm 25

To You, God, I will lift up my soul
In You I will trust; You will be my God, my only God
But I know myself – there is no way I can really do that
Unless You squelch all my tendencies to ignore You
To let my life be ruled by my fears and worries
Instead of by my hope in You
So keep on clearing the path for me, God
Be the gardener and groundskeeper of my mind and heart
Teach me how to control my fears and worries
Teach me Your truth, remind me of Your ability to save me
So that all day, every day, I can live in Your hope and peace
Thankfully, Your mercy and steadfast love are older and stronger
Than my sins and miseries
Just, please, treat me according to Your mercy and steadfast love
Rather than according to my sins and miseries
I'm Your child and, like a loving child, I want to be like You
I want to be good and upright, like You
I want to be humble and content, like You
I want to be loving and faithful, like You
So, again, I pray that You will treat me
Not as if my failings were all there is to me
But as though I truly am like You, made in Your image
I know I envision a good life for my children
So I'm sure You envision a good eternal life for me
But I can't get there unless You clear the path, plow the road
Whisper Your truths to my heart
Help me to remember that my wounds
Those wounds of depression and despair
Discouragement and envy will only heal
Not by my finger probing them again and again
But by applying, again and again, day after day
The healing salve of Your mercy and enduring faithfulness
So I pray with the psalmist
"Turn to me and be gracious to me
For I am lonely and afflicted

The troubles of my heart have multiplied
Free me from my anguish"
To believe in You means to have confidence
That You get it, You know all of the ways
That I feel beaten and overwhelmed
And You want something better for me
You can create something better for me
You can rescue me; in You I can find safety and peace
In Your great castle I can live a life filled with truth and rightness
A life of peace and plenty
Save me, O God of old, God of ages, God of ancient salvation
You save millions, billions
Let me be one of them
Save me from all my troubles. Amen

Psalm 26

I need You to claim me, God
As if I had led a blameless life
As if every day had been a best day
Because on a best day
I trust You without wavering
You can examine my thoughts and feelings
And find only love and Your truth
No lies, no hypocrisy, no envy
No sins, no doubts, no failings at all
Just Your innocence and my worship of You
My life resonates with Your praise
My words and actions reflect Your grace, Your salvation
I love Your place in my soul, that interior castle
Where Your glory dwells
So please, God, make this best the daily reality of my life
Don't let my thoughts, feelings and actions turn dark
Don't let me sink beneath storms of doubt
Don't let me forget
Redeem me and be merciful to me
As if I had led a life without doubt, a life always centered on You
Quiet my storms, level my pits
So I can stand secure in Your peace
So I can praise You with my whole being. Amen

Psalm 27

God is my light and my salvation – What darkness need I fear?
God is my strength – What weakness can destroy me?
When the dark and deadly arise in me to devour my peace
When my doubts and depression attack me
They will not, cannot succeed
Though darkness besieges me, God can lighten my heart
Though those warring nations arise inside me
Even then I can trust God
One thing I ask of God; this is what I seek
That my spirit may ever find
Rest, peace and shelter in God all the days of my life
That my inner vision remain fixed on the strong beauty of God
That my thoughts ever seek God, my Lady Wisdom
Then in my times of trouble God will keep me safe and secure
God will shield me from despair
God will lift me high above depression
Then I will feel exalted, victorious over that creeping darkness
Then I can offer God my joy, my praise, my song, my soul
So, God, please: Hear my voice when I call
Have mercy and answer me
My heart tells me to seek You; help me, God, to follow my heart
Don't give up on me; don't get angry with me
Don't reject or forsake me
O God, my Savior, my Wisdom Woman
Though I sometimes feel forsaken by family, friends
And even by You, God, You keep me close.
So please, teach me Your ways, lead me in Your path
Away from my darkness, away from my doubts and demons
Away from the violence I do to my own peace of mind
So that I can recognize Your goodness all around me
Then I will wait with confidence for You, God
Then I will be strong and take heart and wait – and wait –
Confidently for You, God. Amen

Psalm 28

To You I call, O God, my strong foundation
Do not turn a deaf ear to me
For if You remain silent I will be lost
Lost in the pit of my doubts and darkness
Hear my cry for help, for mercy
As I lift my heart to Your holiness
Do not let me be dragged down by wickedness
Do not let me be good only in how I look to others
While inside my heart turns to evil and malicious thoughts
You and You alone can destroy the darkness in me
Only Your light can banish that darkness
You can tear down the hardened walls around my heart
You can soften my heart as You did Pharaoh's of old
And so I praise You, my God, knowing You have heard me
Truly You are my strength, the shield of my mind
My heart trusts You; my heart leaps for joy
The joy in my heart spills upward into song and praise
I am Yours. You are my strength and shield, my salvation security
You save me, You save us all, You bless us
You shepherd us, You carry us
Forever. Alleluia and Amen!

Psalm 29

In God I find strength, glory and holiness
In God is power, beauty and majesty
Uprooting my weakness and troubles
Breaking down my doubts and denial
When I feel close to God, my heart skips and sings
When I feel close to God, my spirit overflows with joy
When I feel close to God, there is no desert in my soul
There is no forest of confusion
There is no storm of uncertainty
Such relief, to believe in, to know, the power of God
My spirit cries "Glory to God"
God is my sovereign forever; God is my strength forever
God blesses me with peace. Amen

Psalm 30

I will turn my thoughts and my thanks to You, God
For lifting me up, for giving me the grace to live well
I turn to You for help and You heal me
You bring me out of those deadly Ds: depression, despair, doubt
Surrounded by, in harmony with, that great cloud of witnesses
I sing to God, I praise Her holy name
I may feel God's anger at moments
But throughout my life I live in God's steadfast love and grace
I may cry through some nights, but morning always comes
There comes – again and again – those times – those blessed times
When I feel secure, when my faith is strong and solid
When I can live in an awareness of God's grace
When I feel my life is large and strong
But when I am overwhelmed by doubt, I shrink and quake
Then I need Your grace, God, to call to You
As if I have to convince You or remind You
That I cannot praise or appreciate You when I am in that pit of Ds
When I am as if just dust with no divine forever
Again and again I need to call out of the dust of my life
Call out to You for grace and mercy, for help
Help to live joyfully, help to lift up my heart
Help to live in thankfulness to You always. Amen

Psalm 31

In You, God, I take refuge; refuge from my own shame
Deliver me in Your righteousness
Listen, please, to me, and come quickly to my rescue
Be my protecting mother, my saving father
Trusting that You are my mother and father
I know You will lead and guide me
You will keep those internal traps from catching me
From destroying my peace and my abilities
Into Your hands I commit my spirit and my life
Deliver me, my faithful God
Deliver me from worthless idols
Let me always say, "I trust in God"
I will be glad and rejoice in Your steadfast love
For you saw my affliction and knew the anguish of my soul
You have not abandoned me to darkness
You have lifted my spirits into a spacious place
Please, God, be merciful to me when I am in distress
When I feel weak with sorrow
Bowed down in soul and body with grief
When it seems my life is consumed by anguish, my years by groaning
When my own strength of will is not enough
When my resolve weakens
When I feel deserted by friends and neighbors
When I feel dead, broken like discarded pottery
When I feel like my own thoughts conspire against me
Taking everything worthwhile from my life
Then, then, please, let me turn to You, God
Let me say, "I am Yours"
My times are in Your hands, please save me
Let Your face shine on me
Save me through Your steadfast love
Remove my shame, my fear, my self-defeat
Silence the whispers of worthlessness
That destroy my peace with lies
Let me remember this

How abundant are the good things that You have stored up
For those who turn to You, take refuge in You
Shelter in Your presence
Hide in Your dwelling
Safe from darkness and fear
Safe from self-defeat and discouragement
Praise be to You, God,
For You show me the wonders of Your steadfast love
When I felt like a city under siege
When I felt entirely cut off from You
When my trust in You, my belief in You, failed
Still You heard my cry, You saw my need, You saved me
Let me always love God, let me always be faithful
God is strong enough to take care of us all
So I can be strong; I can take heart
I can hope in God. Amen

Psalm 32

I count myself lucky because my sins are forgiven
Covered, not counted, wiped clean
So my spirit, my soul does not need to hide behind lies
When I lie to myself, when I pretend I can rule my own life
I end up depressed, defeated, feeling downtrodden and deserted
I have no energy, no enthusiasm, no stamina, no hope
Then when I remember to turn to You, God
I find renewal and forgiveness
Therefore, let me pray to You always because You are always with me
Through my stormy times, through my desert times
You are my best refuge
You protect me from my troubles, Your power sings within me
Your power sings that You will stay with me
Teach me, counsel me, love me
Help me in my stubbornness
Make me less like a mule and more like a dog.
Help me to remember
That even when I feel overwhelmed by threats to my peace of mind
Overwhelmed by life
Your steadfast love surrounds me, if I just trust in You
So, with that great cloud of witnesses
With all of us redeemed by Your righteousness
I can rejoice and be glad
I can sing and be happy
I can live in Your peace that passes understanding. Amen

Psalm 33

(I read the start of psalm 33 and wondered, why would I sing joyfully? But by the end of the psalm, my heart WAS singing.)

I sing joyfully to God
Though I have only borrowed righteousness
I can do the loud shouts
Not so much the play skillfully
And my song is not a new song
But the old, old song of that great cloud of witnesses
This, this is the God who calls me to Her
God of faithfulness
God of righteousness
God of justice
God of steadfast love
God is my creator and savior
God is my hope and my strength
God's word is strong and true
God's promise is faithful, righteous and just
God's steadfast love is unfailing
The earth is full of God's steadfast love
God created the world: skies, seas, land, every living being
Rulers hold power for a time
God's power is forever
Might can win some battles
God's might conquers all
Sometimes I can do what I want; often I fail
God's plans never fail
God's purpose never waivers
And God's plan, God's purpose, is to love me, to save me
God watches over me, over all of us, forms our hearts
Considers our strengths and weaknesses – with steadfast love
And so we can always wait in hope for God
God who is our help and our shield
God whom we trust, God in whom we rejoice
God whose steadfast love is always with us
God who causes us to sing a new song
A song of hope and love and praise and joy. Amen

Psalm 34
(one of my favorites)

This is how I want to live my life:
Praising God at all time, for the greater glory of God
When I am afflicted with doubts and despair
Let me remember and rejoice
Let me remember that God answers me when I call
God delivers me from all my fears
God makes me glow with happiness and security
God saves me out of all my troubles
God surrounds me with steadfast love and delivers me
Let me taste and see that God is good
Let me be among the blessed with take refuge in God
Let me remember that those who revere God are content
Natural strength and power fail, God's never fails
Like a child, I need to learn this lesson again and again
(I write the psalms to teach myself this lesson)
Like everyone, I love life and want many good days
I want success and contentment and love
God instructs me, in love, in the right way
The way of truth, the way of goodness, the way of peace
Let me seek peace and pursue it always
God sees the goodness in me; God supports the goodness in me
God turns away my depression, doubts, despair
God delivers me from all my troubles
When I am brokenhearted, when my spirit feels crushed
Even then God is close, God saves me
God lends me Her own righteousness
God protects my life and my spirit, my soul and my heart
Evil and wickedness, doubt and despair will disappear
God will never disappear
My rescue is assured, my refuge is safe, forever. Amen

Psalm 35

God, you know my enemies
I do not have to worry about war or life-threatening illness
I do not have to worry about people wanting to kill me
You know what kills my spirit
What threatens my faith and contentment
You know my terrible Ds: doubt, depression, despair, discouragement
You know how often my own thoughts and worries defeat me
How often I say, "This is too much", "I can't", "I'm not good enough"
These are the enemies I need You to contend with for me
Come to my aid with all Your weapons of salvation and steadfast love
Turn away my downtrodden thoughts and feelings
Let them blow away on Your mighty wind
Don't let them overtake me, trip me up, bury me
Let me rejoice in You, let me praise You to the skies
Let me find my confidence and peace in You
Rescue and enrich my poor soul
Rescue me from my own tendencies to rob my confidence
When those thoughts of being unworthy fill me
When I question the value of everything I have done
When I feel unloved, unnoticed, unworthy
When I begin to compare myself, always unfavorably, with others
Rescue me, save me, grant me Your peace that passes understanding
Lift me up so that all can see my great thanksgiving to You
Save me from my own turmoil, doubts and confusion
Do not be far from me, God
Save me through Your righteousness
Save me from my monsters that swallow my possibilities
My friends will join me in praising You
In shouting for joy and gladness
We will say, "God, who ensures our well-being, be exalted"
I will proclaim YOUR righteousness
Sing YOUR praises all day long. Amen

Psalm 36

God's message is in my heart
Even more than in a book or a church
God warns me about the futility of going my own way
Of ignoring God
When I flatter myself, when I rely on myself,
When I regard my independence with pride
That is exactly when I am most blind
When I brag, when I focus on getting my own way
That is when I lie awake at night, feeling lost, feeling like a fake
I lose my way, I can't tell right from wrong
Then, once again, You save me, O God
Your steadfast love reaches to the heavens – and to my depths
Your enduring faithfulness is wider than the skies
Your righteousness is higher and stronger
Than my mountain of doubt
Your love, Your steadfast love, O God is priceless and precious
I can take refuge in the shadow of Your wings
I can feast on the abundance of Your gracious bounty
I can drink from Your river of delights
From Your wellspring of eternal life
In Your light, I see light; In Your light I live life eternal
Continue Your loving attention that I may not forget You
Let Your righteousness take root in my heart
Let Your righteousness grow ever stronger in me
Strangling the pride, crowding out the doubt,
Burying the discouragement
Let Your righteousness be my guard against sin. Amen

Psalm 37

God, help me to not fret over my shortcomings
Or keep thinking I am inferior
Those that I envy are no better than me
They are just as mortal, just as sinful
Grant me peace of mind that I may trust in You
That I may do good, enjoy my life
Let me delight in You
And remember that my truest desires are centered in You
Let me commit – again and again – to You
And trust that You will give me my true desires
Let Your righteousness be mine, shining with dawn's new light
Let Your justice be mine, shining with noon's bright glare
Let Your peace be mine, shining with evening's gentle glow
Still my restless soul that I may wait patiently for You
Without worry or anxiety, without dread or envy
Help me to turn from anger and wrath, from all that is bad for my spirit
You will triumph over all my faults
You will bless my trust with a place in Your kingdom
A little while You promise, and I will struggle no more
You will banish and vanish my faults, my terrible Ds
So, trusting in Your greatness, I will live peacefully
With meekness in Your grace
I may feel torn new
Like a battle between good and evil rages within me and I am losing
But You, God, simply laugh at my terrible foes
You know they are no match for You
My battle rages on, the enemies of my peace seem powerful
And threaten to conquer me
But You, God, conquer them, You destroy the destroyers
"Better one day in Your courts than thousands elsewhere"
Better what seems to be Your little
Than deceitful tumultuous longings, envy, wealth and ease
For the power of dis-ease is broken by the might of Your righteousness
You brings days of peace, an everlasting inheritance of goodness
Even when I feel empty or embattled
Your righteousness and steadfast love do not desert me
What to me seems like strong choking weeds smothering my peace

Will wither before Your power
They will vanish like smoke, burned up by Your righteousness
When I am fearful, I get selfish
But when I trust in You, God, I love being generous
Because I remember my rich inheritance through Your blessings
I remember that You guard and firm my path
When I walk trusting in Your steadfast love
Even when I stumble into darkness, Your light will find me
Your strength will lift me up again and again
I was young and now I am old; I was full of faith and then empty
I was hopeful and then despairing
But, though I did not always know it
Never was I deserted by You, God
You help me to be generous to others
You bless my children and their children
So I can turn from my inner struggles and look outward to do good
Working in Your kingdom forever
You love justice; You are faithful; You protect me
You cut off my doubts and despair
You bequeath Your own righteousness to me
You grant me rights to Your divine eternal kingdom
Because of You, I can be righteousness
I can speak with wisdom and justice
I can keep Your peace and justice in my heart, letting it guide me
Doubt and despair may still contend for my soul, for my peace
But You will not leave me in their power or let them condemn me
Let me wait for You, God, and keep Your way
And I will inherit Your kingdom and see the end of my troubles
Although I may feel like trouble is winning in my life
In Your time it will soon pass away and be no more
Here is what I want to remember always:
There is future – God's eternal future – for the person of peace
There is no future for doubt, despair, depression, envy
Or any trouble that destroys God's peace
Salvation begins with God's righteousness
God is my stronghold in time of trouble
God helps me, delivers me, save me – not because of my goodness
But because I take refuge in Her. Amen

Psalm 38

When I am down, when those terrible Ds attack
Then, God, I feel like You are against me
I feel unwanted, unloved, abandoned, wounded with a deadly wound
Nothing feels good or healthy; I feel weak in my very bones
My guilt – real and imagined – overwhelms me
A burden too heavy to bear
I imagine myself as something foul and rotting, too sick to be healed
I am bowed down, brought low, going through my days with no joy
So heavy feels my burden that my back aches
My joints stiffen, my skin is on fire
I feel feeble, crushed, I groan with anguish in my heart
But You know all of this, none of this is news to You
Weakness and darkness – that is my world
Loneliness and rejection – that is my world
Failure and doubt – that is my world
Deaf to pleasure, mute in praise – that is my reality
Deaf to joy, mute in thanksgiving – that is my reality
Waiting, waiting, not able to do anything
I wait for You to rescue me – again
As always I ask that You save me from myself
Pick me up before I slip down completely into a silent, dark grave
The most I can do is find the ability, in my pain and despair and doubt
To ask You, who may not exist, to do it for me
The most I can do is admit all I can't do for myself
When I am losing the battle against the enemies of my peace of mind
When my life seems useless
When everything I try to do seems worthless
When failure rules my thoughts
Do not forsake me, God, do not withdraw from me
Though I withdraw from You
Come quickly then to help me, O God my Savior. Amen

Psalm 39

Over and over I promise myself
That I will control my temper and my tongue
I will put a muzzle on my mouth when I am hurt or angry
But then I hurt by my silent withdrawal
Not even saying anything good
And meanwhile my hurt and anger grow hotter and hotter within me
I try to pray, to meditate but the fire burns inside me until I explode
Then I turn on You, God, and demand that You help me
Humble me, bring me back to the reality of how short life is
How little time we each really have, the good as well as the bad
How foolish we are to rush around being upset by this life
Its riches and disappointments, its honors and hurts
When all will vanish and only You will remain
What can I look for, hope for, but You; my hope is in You
Only You can save me from myself
Only You can give me worthy words, worthy thoughts, worthy feelings
You take away all pretense, all worthless strivings
All false philosophies
Before Your eternalness, everyone's life is but a breath
So hear my prayer, God, listen to my cry for help
Do not be deaf to my weeping
Although I often feel that You are distant and unknowable
Although I sometimes doubt that You are real
Although I may feel as pagan as any Gentile of old
Please accept me, don't be angry with me, save me
That I may enjoy life in this world before I depart it forever. Amen

Psalm 40

I wait patiently for You, God, to turn to me and hear my cry
I wait for You to lift me out of this slimy pit of sadness
Out of the mud and mire of gloom and discouragement
I wait for You to set my feet on the strong foundation of Your salvation
To give me a firm place to stand in Your peace
I wait for You to put a new song in my heart and mouth
A glad song of praise to You
I would like people to look at me and see You,
Your **steadfast** love and **enduring** faithfulness shining through
So they will know to trust their happiness to You
Blessed will I be when I trust You that way
When I do not look to my own prideful accomplishments
When I do not put my faith in the idols of this world
Help me, God
To remember the wonders You have already done for me
Help me, God, to trust the good You have planned for me
Help me, God, to remember that none can compare with You
For Your goodness and righteousness is too great
To tell or comprehend
Help me, God, to remember that You want ME,
Not my money or possessions, but my love and trust in You
You don't want a hollow "I'm sorry" but You do want to hear me say
"Here I am, I have come; I desire to do your will, my God
I desire to have Your law within my heart"
Help me, God, to proclaim by my life Your saving acts
Help me, God, to treasure Your righteousness in my heart
Help me, God, to speak of Your **enduring** faithfulness and saving help
Do not withhold Your mercy from me, God
May Your **steadfast** love and **enduring** faithfulness always protect me
You know how often I feel that troubles without number surround me
How often I feel that there is no hope, no peace, no goodness in me
How often I can't stop the negative, hurtful thoughts and feelings
How often my heart, my courage, my optimism, fail me
Be pleased to save me, God; come quickly, God, to help me
Let all the negatives disappear before Your great positive
Let all the despair drown in Your great hope

Let all the dark discouragement vanish
In the light of Your steadfast love
Let me, with all who seek You, rejoice and be glad in You
Let me, with all who long for Your saving help, always say
"God is great!"
But for all that, here I sit, poor and needy, again and again, needy
Think of me, please, God
For You alone are my help and my deliverer
You alone are my God
So, please, come quickly, do not delay. Amen

Psalm 41

Blessed, blessed, when I remember others before myself
Let me care for and be one of the so-called weak
Let me rely on God to deliver me from troubles
Let me rely on God to protect and preserve me
Let me rely on God to bless me
Let me remember that God does not abandon me to my fears
Let me remember that God sustains me through all woes
Let me remember that God restores me despite any weakness
Have mercy on me, God, heal me, for I am full of sorrow
I feel deserted, maligned, afraid, cast off, alone
Will anyone notice when I die? Will anyone care?
Whom can I trust? Whom can I turn to?
I know that my friends and family deserve better from me
And yet I feel alone and fearful
As if no one cares, as if everyone thinks I am worthless
As if even my best friends have given up on me
Because I have given up on myself
But may You, God, have mercy on me
Raise me up
Remind me that You are pleased with me
Remind me that no enemy triumphs over You
And You are within me; You uphold me
You set me in Your presence forever
Praise be to God from everlasting to everlasting
Amen and Amen

A Riff on Psalm 42

What do I know about deer? Only that there are too many of them
They keep getting killed by cars and trucks
But I know about dry and thirsty souls
Feeling that my mind is parched, my soul is shriveled
Was it P, P & M who sang about the woman at the well?
"Jesus met the woman at the well…
She went running, crying, 'God help me.'"
I'm a woman, dry and thirsty, at Your well of eternal water
God, help me
I can't say that I cry – even crying is too active
I can't even say that I am waiting
I'm just kind of hibernating, shriveling, longing
Trying to remember what it felt like to be confident
To feel blessed, under Your protection, Mighty Wisdom Woman,
To join others with songs and shouts of joy and praise
It's not like it was long ago – there are moments, more than moments
When I live even now within that joy and hope and friendship
But then why do I still get so downcast? Why so parched again?
Why so disturbed within myself? Why so hopeless?
Back and forth I go, between hope and despair, between love and loss
"Deep calls to deep", the psalmist says
"All Your waves and breakers have swept over me"
Some days I feel You with me, some nights I'm content
Your song and prayer fill my life
Then again I start feeling like You have forgotten me
That there is nothing in my life but mourning and regret
Oppressed by my own doubts, feeling more dead than alive
Questioning, doubting, crying, Where are You, God?
Why do I struggle so, again and again?
Why is my peace of mind so fragile?
Give me Your everlasting water, that I may never thirst again
And the psalmist tells me
Put your hope in God for you will yet praise God
God, your Savior. Amen

Psalm 43

I ask You, O God, once again – again and again –
Help me, defend me, save me, here on earth
As You have done for eternity
Save me from deceitful distractions
Deliver me from unworthy interests
You are God – mighty over all
So if I can't depend on You to help me
What hope do I have?
So help me already
I'm tired, weary of walking about as if in mourning,
Weary of feeling as if I am oppressed by an enemy,
When I am my own enemy, always
O God, my God, blind me to the world
Blind me with your blazing truth
Let your truth lead me, your beauty guide me
Let me look at the world, let me live my life
As if from atop Your holy hill
As if worshipping always at Your altar
Let me laugh with the joy of Your service; sing with Your praise
(Never mind that I can't carry a tune; You don't care so I won't either)
Stop feeling sorry for yourself, O my soul, stop your grumbling
Stop feeling you need to be something more
Stop regretting you aren't special, aren't more talented, aren't a saint
God wants what you are, not what you are not.
So just put your hope, your faith, your joy, your life in God
Who is Lady Wisdom
Praise God, your help. Amen .

Psalm 44

I remember, or try to remember, what You have already done for me
How many times You lifted me up out of depression, despair, doubt
Lifted me to the peace of dry land above the floods of my anguish
How many times You freed me from my guilt and discouragement
I didn't win through by my own marvelous intellect
Or serene self-confidence or glowing health
You won through for me
It was Your light that dispelled my darkness
Your face that was the day sun driving down the deep night
Help me, help me, help me again, now and always
Today and tomorrow
And tomorrow and tomorrow and tomorrow,
To remember that You are my Sovereign, my God, my Wisdom Woman
Through You, in Your name, I live well
Not necessarily happily but well
No human philosophies, no latest remedies can save me
Only You, Only You, Only You
I will give thanks to Your name forever
I have been feeling abandoned, as though You rejected me
Refused to fight my enemies, gave up on me
Left me in darkness and despair, scattered and shattered my peace
So I disappoint myself and others
All day long my disgrace is before me and shame covers my face
I hide in my bed, on my sofa, in my electronic world
What did I do, what did I fail to do, how am I at fault
Did I decide to turn from You? I don't think so.
Did I reject You, doubt You
 (Well, yes, OK, I doubted, but that is nothing new)
Come on, God, You know me
It's not like my doubts and failings are news to You
So, please, please, please, rouse Yourself. Wake up
Take me back, let Your face be my sun again
Don't forget me, don't let me sink into the dust of my terrible Ds
Rise up, come to my help
Redeem me, yet again and always, for the sake of Your steadfast love
Amen and Thank You

Psalm 45

Here's a psalm of joy and celebration; here's an ode to banished Ds
In You, O God, in faith, in love, my heart overflows
In You I feel blessed forever; You are my strength and my beauty
You give me victory
Over doubt, despair, depression, darkness, danger, denial, even death
You pierce my heart with love and in that piercing
Those deadly internal enemies die
Your glory and majesty become my own
Your throne, O God, endures forever and ever
Your justice is Your scepter
You are crowned with righteousness
All of our images, our poor Disney images
Of kings and queens, princes and princesses
Pale before the reality of Your everlasting majesty
You are the reality
The rest, even the "real" earthly royalty, are pretenders
Imitators, shadows in this shadowland
But if You are Sovereign and we are Your children
Then we too are royalty
Through You, because of You
We bow to You and You lift us up
With joy and gladness we are led to You – led by Your mercy
So we enter Your palace, the palace of our Sovereign Parent
We are Yours, O Sovereign from eternity
Sovereign from always, for always
You have made us Your children
We will celebrate Your Name in all generations
We will praise You forever and ever. Amen

Psalm 46

God is my refuge and strength, an ever present help in trouble
Even when I don't know it, can't recognize it
Therefore, I do not have to fear
Though my life changes and changes again
Though the mountain of my faith sinks
In the tumultuous seas of my doubts
Though my doubts roar and foam into despair
Though my faith trembles
Still, through my life the river of God's grace flows fresh and sure
Whenever I let myself drown in it, I arise baptized again in gladness
Knowing I am destined for God's own heaven
God is in the midst of my life and God will not let go of me
God's help dawns ever new in my life
My world tumbles around me again and again
My sureness in my own self totters
I stumble, I fall, my own earth quakes, my doubts flood me
Then I remember, then I feel it again:
God, God almighty, is with me
God, God is with me no less than with my ancestors
Because somehow, by some miracle
I am part of that great cloud of witnesses
So come and see me – me, a work of God
See how God desolates my terrible Ds
See how God causes all those wars inside me to still to peace
See how God destroys all the weapons that destroy my peace
God commands my internal turmoil,
"Be still! Be still and know that I am God
Exalted among all people; exalted in all your life
Exalted and lifting you with Me above all your troubles
God, God of forever and everyone, God of power, is with me
God is with me no less than with my ancestors
Because somehow, by some miracle
I am part of that great cloud of witnesses. Amen

Psalm 47

I will laugh, I will clap my hands, I will make noise enough for nations
God, hear my joy; God, know that I rejoice today, tonight in You
You are awesome; Sovereign of my world; Crusher of my doubts
Light to my darkness; Parent to my child; Giver to my needs
Lover to myself, my whole self, even the parts that I don't love
Ha, God has blessed me and blessed me and blessed me
God is on top of my world; God is Conqueror of my troubles
God is Sovereign and God ENJOYS my singing! Ha! So there
I will sing and sing and sing to my Sovereign and God will smile
I sing because God is Sovereign, God is holy, God is all I need
From my lowest thoughts and troubles to my highest works and loves
From my worst to my best: God is Sovereign, God reigns over all
I belong to God – all of me; I don't have to disown any of me
God loves me and God is greatly exalted. Amen and Hallelujah!

Psalm 48

I begin with the end, for the sheer beauty and joy of it
"For this God is our God for ever and ever;
[S]he will be our guide even to the end."
The psalmist gets there through imagery that is foreign to me
Zaphon, Mount Zion, Tarshish, the villages of Judah
These I do not know
But I know the praise, I know the assurance, I know the joy
The joy of having a Savior
The assurance that our God conquers evil
The praise of such unfailing might – on our side!
And so, I can echo the psalmist: God makes me secure forever
And then, and then, with the psalmist:
"Within your temple, O God,
We meditate on your steadfast love.
Like your name, O God,
Your praise reaches to the end of the earth;
Your right hand is filled with righteousness."
I rejoice, I am glad, I tell of your wonders
And so, here I am, back at the end
This is our God forever and ever, our Guide to the end. Amen

Psalm 49

Ah, how many are my parts; "I contain multitudes"
The good, the bad, the beautiful, the ugly
The serene, the conflicted, the faithful, the doubt-filled
I want to choose wisdom and understanding
I want to depend on God's wisdom, to sing my doubts away
So much competes for my attention, so many promises
Promises of happiness, wealth, health, success, nirvana even
I can get myself twisted in knots, trying to discern truth
Until, like jesting Pilate, I wash my hands of it all
Because nothing is worthwhile, nothing truly holds the secret
No practice, no philosophy, no promise, no purpose
Nothing redeems my life, nothing guarantees eternal life
My wisdom will count for nothing, my foolishness will be forgotten
My wealth will not buy life, my poverty will not guarantee goodness
Yoga will not give me youth; prayers will not earn me years
In the end, like all animals, I will die
Death is my shepherd
Wait – wait – Death WAS my shepherd but no longer has to be
"I am the shepherd," said Jesus
My Christ, my God-Anointed, God-Appointed One
"I am the way, the truth, the life"
Can there be any other answer? Can wealth suffice? Happiness? Wisdom?
Do they last beyond death?
Ah, no, the psalmist reminds us
Humans like animals must die
Nothing accumulated on earth is permanent, all will pass away.
If we are to be more than animals, if we are to survive death
We must look beyond earth. Amen

Psalm 50

God, my God, summons me, calls upon me to pay attention
Not just on Sunday, not just for a few minutes of prayer
But all day, every day, from dawn to dawn, God wants me
God wants me to recognize the beauty, the perfection
The perfect beauty of what She has to give
God speaks, but can I hear, even though God speaks mightily
God calls, but do I answer, even though God is my Judge
God asks, but how do I respond to God's righteousness
What need does God have of my church-going, my prayer-recitals
What can I bring to God that God does not already have
God created the universe, God does not need anything from me
I, on the other hand, need everything from God
If I am to have any righteousness, any holiness, any salvation
Then it will only be as a gift from God, not from my efforts
My only duty is to recognize my helplessness, turn to God
With thanksgiving and praise
Then God will take care of those terrible Ds for me
God will cast them out as Jesus cast out devils
I will laugh and be free because God can do what I cannot
God knows the good and the bad, the worthy and the unworthy of me
God knows the struggle and the quiet, the faith and the doubt of me
God knows the gratitude and the envy
The generosity and the meanness of me
God knows it all and can take care of it all
So I will come, come as one of the faithful
With thanksgiving to honor God, my Lady Wisdom
God who clears my mind and heart of the terrible Ds
God who gives me a clear path to Her
God who saves me. Amen

Psalm 51

Have mercy on me, O God of steadfast love
O God of great compassion
Blot out my troublesome doubts and despair
Wash away all my dark thoughts
Cleanse my selfish feelings
For I know my worst tendencies
They are always before me
They lead me away from Your peace and light
Into turmoil and darkness
I begin to doubt and fear Your righteousness, Your judgment
It becomes easier to believe that You don't exist
That You are a creation of human beings
I am not alone in this, surely
It seems to be pretty common among all people
This turning from You
Yet You remain
From before I was, from when I first was
Through my life and past it
The psalmist says that You taught us wisdom
In the secret place of the womb
Maybe, but I forget it too easily
In the public places of my life
So I'm back asking for Your compassion
Wash away my mind's dark stains
Let my thoughts turn to rejoicing, to joy, to gladness
Help me to turn away, as You turn away
From darkness and selfishness
"Create in me a pure heart, O God,
And renew a steadfast spirit within me"
Don't desert me; don't let me forget that I need You
"Restore to me the joy of Your salvation"
Turn my self-centered pride into a God-centered willing spirit
That will sustain me
Then maybe, just maybe, I can remember You in my dark times
I can turn back to You when I feel low and unloved

When I feel defeated by my own negativity, hurt and anger
Deliver me from my crushing feelings of inadequacy and despair
O God, You are my Savior, my only hope
Let my mind and heart sing of Your righteousness
Then my words, my life will reflect Your goodness, will declare Your praise
You do not delight in my fears, my withdrawal from life
You take no pleasure in watching me undermine myself
I will draw away from doubt and despair, from selfishness and pride
I will come to You for peace and security, for **steadfast** love and hope
May it please You to draw me ever more into Your castle
Ever nearer to Your bright throne
Surrounded by Your great glowing cloud of witnesses
I can let Your light devour my darkness. Amen

Psalm 52

Why do I take pride in the wrong things
And think myself better than others?
I fool myself, I tear myself down by such thoughts
I get everything backwards
I value the worthless and throw away the precious
Too easily my thoughts become words
Disparaging words, hurtful words, that can't be unsaid
God, Sovereign Wisdom Woman, You can stop me
You can turn me from such thoughts
You can give me Your righteousness
So that I can laugh at myself, appreciate my own absurdity
Do I want to depend upon the strength of money and reputation
Both of which can be stolen and destroyed?
Or, like the olive tree, do I want to flourish
By drawing life and strength from God's unfailing richness
From God's **steadfast** love forever and ever
Do this for me, please God, that I may praise You forever
Hoping always in Your name, trusting always in Your **steadfast** love
Flourishing always in Your goodness, praising You always. Amen

Psalm 53

Sometimes I foolishly stop believing, telling myself there is no god
But then I just seem to sink lower and lower
Thankfully, God is patient, waiting for me to once again turn around
My own repeated metanoia
While I, I go my own way, stumbling blindly forward
Finding goodness harder and harder, more elusive, more uncertain
Will I never learn? Will I ever stop letting doubt devour my peace, my faith?
Here I stand – in all the rich irony of that
Overwhelmed with dread when there is nothing to dread
God scatters my doubt
God turns me around
Oh, that God would keep being God, keep saving me
Keep restoring the fortune of my faith
Let me rejoice and be glad in that certain salvation. Amen

Psalm 54

Save me, O God, by Your name; vindicate me by Your might
Hear my prayer, O God, listen to the words of my mouth
Strange thoughts and fantasies, strange worries and fears
Attack my peace of mind
My life turns from You
Surely You will help me; surely You can turn me back
Banish those unhelpful, negative thoughts and feelings
In Your enduring faithfulness, restore my faith, my peace
Let me live my life honoring You, praising You, giving You credit
For You have delivered me – time and time again – from all my troubles
I can examine my life without fear
Because of Your great power, mercy and steadfast love. Amen

Psalm 55

[First, thank You, God, that I prayed Psalm 5 and Psalm 55 this morning. You brought me through a challenging day. Please grant me restful sleep, peace and patience tomorrow.]

Listen to me, God, don't ignore me, hear my need and answer it
For I am troubled and uneasy
As always, my negative thoughts – about myself and others
Undermine my peace, give rise to anger, cause me pain
My world turns dark and deadly, I lose joy, I find only discontent
I imagine life would be better, easier, more worthwhile
If I were different
If I were some place different, if others changed
I imagine I can outrun my storms
That's hopeless. I have only one real hope: You, God, You
You are my hope, my salvation
You can bring beauty and peace, order out of chaos
Strength to my interior castle
You can make it worthy of Your throne
The parts of myself that I value most
My intellect, my compassion even
These can turn against me when I use them in pride
When I use them to convince myself I am better than others
Let those tendencies die for they are evil within me
Let me call to You, God, my Lady Wisdom, instead
Admitting my weakness, my powerlessness
Evening, morning and noon, help me to turn to You
To remember that You hear me, You help me
You ransom me unharmed
Though my own thoughts try to defeat me, depress me
God, Almighty Wisdom Woman, You and You alone can help me change
You and You alone can teach me to revere You
Oh, I can tell myself fine stories of my understanding
Of my superiority
I can smooth over my faults but they are killing me
So I need You, my savior God, to sustain me
To uphold what is best in me
To defeat what is worst, to rid me of all that is not good for me
I trust You. Amen

Psalm 56

Have mercy on me, Oh God, for my dark tendencies pursue me
All day long they try to undermine my peace
I am afraid that my own failures, my own harshness about others
My own pride will condemn me
What can I do except rely on You?
You, my God, whose word I praise.
In You I can trust and not be afraid.
What can even I do that You cannot forgive and overcome?
You know how I struggle, how I feel attacked, betrayed, harmed
Trapped by my own darkness and doubt
I fear for my eternal life
Please, please, help me, save me
Don't let me disappear into my own darkness
What do I have to offer You except my tears
(not even blood, toil and sweat – just tears)
My dark enemies will vanish in Your light
You, my God, whose Word I praise
You, my God, whose Word I praise
In You I can trust and not be afraid
What can even I do that You cannot forgive and overcome
I want to be faithful to You, God
I want to live thankfully not fearfully
I want to remember that You have delivered me from death
You keep me from stumbling into pits of my own making
So that I walk before You in the Light of Your Eternal Life. Amen

Psalm 57

Have mercy on me, O God, have mercy
For in You my soul takes refuge
I will take refuge in the shadow of Your wings when disaster threatens
I cry out to You, God most high, help me live Your purpose for me
You came from heaven to save me, saving me from my terrible Ds
You – in steadfast love and enduring faithfulness
I feel like I am in the midst of ravenous lions – and that's when I am alone
My peace of mind is shattered as if by spears and arrows
My own tongue can be like a sharp sword
What a contrast my moaning and troubles are
To Your exalted place of peace
O God, Lady Wisdom, above the heavens
Your glory is wide enough to cover me, to hide me
Yet I feel trapped in a net of my own making
Bowed down by my faults, sinking into a pit of doubt and despair
Please give me a steadfast heart, O God,
Let me sing and make music with a light heart
Awake, oh my soul, awake, sweet music of my soul
Awake to dawning Light
God of Light, I want to praise You all my days: days that You have blessed
For great is Your steadfast love, reaching beyond heaven and earth
Beyond life and death, beyond right and wrong
Great is Your enduring faithfulness, staying beyond my doubts
So You are exalted, O God, Lady Wisdom, above the heavens
Your glory wide enough to hide me. Amen

Psalm 58

I know, God, that there is little justice in my judgments
Pettiness, spite, envy, narrow-mindedness, fear
Misunderstanding, hurt, anger, simple tiredness
Too often these are the enemies of fairness and love
Too often my judgments of others, and myself
Are like a snake's venom
Like a lion's ripping teeth
Please, God, wash away these unjust and unworthy judgments
Blunt them, crush, them, still them
Sweep them away in the flood of Your righteousness
Then I can be glad in Your salvation of all
Your **steadfast** love for all, even me
Then again I will testify all my days
Surely there is a God who judges the earth and saves us all. Amen

Psalm 59

Ah, again, God, please – You know well what I need
I am weak but You are strong; I am child but You are God
So deliver me already, bring me back to You
Defend me from my own darkness
The darkness that wants to eat my life, swallow my faith
Always, always, it lies in wait, just beyond my last prayer
When I choose mindless entertainment over thoughtful peace
When I wander in my purpose, my thoughts, my life
When I lie in bed, sleepless at night, reluctant to wake in the morning
When those dark and dangerous Ds overwhelm me
When I feel sorry for myself – what have I done to deserve this?
Don't I get easy happiness? Don't I get lasting peace?
Don't I get to love and be loved?
You are God, aren't You? Mighty God of Sarah and Ruth, Esther and Mary
So rouse Yourself and do – again – for me what I cannot do for myself
Night after night, day after day, I feel attacked and deserted
My thoughts taste sour; my feelings sting like nettles
I give up
But You, You never give up. You, You, if I could only remember
Remember to watch for You, go to You
Where is my strength, where is my resolve, where is my memory
Gone, all gone
God, God, God, please, please, please, come
Defeat my darkness with Your light
But let me remember the darkness so that I may know
Know that my only safety is hiding in You
Destroy my lies, destroy my pity, destroy my doubts, destroy my pride
Destroy my despair, destroy my anger, destroy my aloneness
Let me know, now and forever, that You rule over my life
Ah, but I will forget, won't I? I will descend, again, to the tomb
I will wallow, I will sludge, I will drown, I will moan
And You will have to rescue me again
Once and for all, Hebrews says. You did it once and for all
But for me it is one more time, again and again
After my night, comes Your dawn

You open my eyes to see Your light again
You open my mouth to sing Your song again
You open my life to live Your grace again
You are my strength, I sing praise to You
You are my God, my fortress and my Wisdom Woman
You are God, on You I rely. Amen

Psalm 60

Old images speak to me of God being elsewhere
Anywhere but with me
I may not know the geography, but I know the feeling
I thought You would win all my battles for me, God
Forever, once and for all
I thought You would conquer my enemies, banish them
So that I would be at peace always, living in Your sight, Your light
But, no, oh no, instead I am left to wonder where You have gone
Why You leave me to the merciless mercy of my demons and darkness
Come on, God, if You're angry with me, get over it
You haven't given up on me, have You?
Left me to desperation, to drown in my sorrows
To truthquakes and night terrors
Save me, help me
Let me revel in the light of Your steadfast love for me
And mine for You
Let me live in landscapes shaped by Your might, Your right
Your steadfast love, Your salvation
If not You, then who? If not in Your presence, then where?
If not by Your strength and righteousness, then how?
Answer me, I beg You for I am worthless in this battle
Alone, I am already defeated
But with You, with You, I will claim victory
I will plant Your peace
When You trample the weeds of my mind. Amen

Psalm 61

Who are You, God?
A person who answers my prayers?
A strong foundation?
A refuge?
A tower?
A tent?
A winged creature?
My benefactor?
YHWH, the great I Am Who I Am?
I pray but I'm not sure Whom it is I pray to
Someday one image speaks to me
Someday another
Someday none
The old images, the old words
I cry out, my heart grows faint
I don't ask to be queen, to be enthroned forever
But I do ask for peace
I turn to You to heal me of my dissatisfactions with myself
Can a strong foundation, a tower, a tent, a winged creature heal me?
I need a Person who will love me faithfully
Of that Person I will sing forever
That Person I will love forever
Or at least as long as She gives me the power to love and sing. Amen

Psalm 62

The story of my life: contradictions and ephemeral certainties
I call on God as if She existed
I put my life in Her hands, proclaim Her my only certainty
I believe, I believe in the Almighty
Who can rule my unruly heart as completely as the ordered cosmos
But but but
Time and again I feel besieged, lost, bewildered
Resentful, deserted, unsure, foolish, alone
Worthless, defeated, deceived, deadened
Are my tears maudlin or spirit-filled
Is my heart naïve or uplifted
How I wish God would grant me continuing certainty
Here is where I want to live: where I can say every day
My soul finds rest in God, my hope arises from God
God is my strong foundation, my salvation, my security
My sure bet, my certainty
I will not be shaken
I know the truth and the truth is God
God is my trustworthy refuge, always
Why can't I hold onto it? Why do I envy just about everyone
Why does my heart turn again and again to the worthless things
To the dark things, to the trivial, to the vain, to the small and mean
And to top it all off, I can't even get past the basic contradiction
That is God
This God in whom I chose to believe
Even though I am uncertain of Her existence
Sometimes, when I turn to God, I know Her power and **steadfast** love
Her ability and willingness to keep me in Her peace
And sometimes when I turn to God, I fear Her judgment
I fear that I can never be what She want, what She deserves.
Aw, hell. Amen

Psalm 63

"Oh God, you are my God, I see you, my soul thirsts for you"
Can't say better than that
Water, water again, the water of eternal life, of no more thirst
The water that causes life to flower
The water of love that is better than life, better than a parched, dry life
In what sanctuary do I find water? Where do I go?
When I lift my hands and one leg in the tree asana?
When I sing hymns in church?
When I sit in bed, early in the morning, playing with the psalms?
Everywhere and anywhere, of course
Here is laughter, here is joy, here is security
Not just water but a rich feast of comfort and security
Morning, noon and night
In waking, working hours, in dark, quiet hours
Always You, God, are my help and in Your shadow is light
And truth and water and feast – joy upon joy
A flood of trouble cannot drown me because You hold onto me
Ha, ha – I laugh the laugh of scorn at troubles, doubts
All the terrible Ds
They are doomed
I am saved. Enough already. Amen

Psalm 64

Hear my voice, O God, raised again in complaint
I know I whine – forgive me but hear me and help me
Keep my peace, conquer my worries
Help me to live in goodness not wickedness
Help me to give love not hate
Help me to be tender not biting
Help me to be joyful not bitter
Don't let me be overtaken, overpowered by envy
Don't let me be ensnared by jealousy or worry
Keep me from hopelessness
Keep me from pride
Keep me from deviousness
Destroy those destroyers of my peace, Oh God
Ruin them, run them out, reverse their plans
And then, and then, lend me Your righteousness
That I can rejoice in You, take refuge in You
Remain steadfast and upright in glorifying You. Amen

Psalm 65

God, most high and excellent Creator, Redeemer, Sustainer
Wisdom Woman
God, today I come to You in joy and gladness
With promises of faithfulness
With gratitude for answered prayer
I come to You as we all come, whether we know it or not
When life overwhelms me
When my own treacherousness betrays my happiness
When I can't forgive myself
YOU FORGIVE ME!!!!!
Laughing and happy, I come with Your great cloud of witnesses
I come because there is nowhere better
I come because with You, in Your goodness and righteousness
Is where I find peace
Because You, in Your mighty righteousness, You have saved me
Delivered me
Given me hope
Just as You created the mountains
Just as You silenced the stormy seas
Just as You have given Your creatures peace and salvation
You created me, You quieted my fears, You give me peace
Wherever I am, I can see Your glory and Your joy in Your creation
In the beauty of sunrise and sunset
In water: rain and rivers, oceans and snow, streams and mists
In the earth: furrows and ridges, pastures and hills, meadows and valleys
With Your good creation
I will shout and sing for the joy of knowing You. Amen

Psalm 66

HA! This is what I call my singing: making a joyful noise to God
I sing because I love to sing – off-key often, wrong words frequently
But I trust that God hears my singing as praise
As gratitude for Her power to vanquish those enemies
That populate my internal world, those terrible Ds
So that ALL of me can praise God. Please & Praise
Ah, I hope I can remember what God has done for me
Time and time again
When I was drowning in doubt, God dried up my doubt
When I slip in my muddy thoughts and murky feelings
God raises me up to worship
God guards me so that darkness does not swallow me. Please & Praise
So let me bless God, let me go on singing Her praise
God, who has kept me from the death of hope
God, who is not afraid to let me fail, let me wait
God, who infuriates me and refuses to baby me
God, who trusts me to survive all of my own troubles
God, who watches as I am burned by doubt, drowned by depression
God, who waits for me, as I wait for Her
In my spacious space of peace
Let me remember God when I am NOT troubled
Let me remember God when my interior world is peaceful
Let me remember then to praise God
To bring my best to God. Please & Praise
Let me remember to tell myself, often, what God has done for me
What God is
Why I believe, even though I doubt and do not believe
Why I love God, even though I doubt and do not believe
Why I rely on God, even though I doubt and do not believe
Why I trust God, even though I distrust most religion
Blessed be God, who has not rejected me
Or removed Her steadfast love from me
Though I doubt and disbelieve and distrust
Blessed be God. Amen

Psalm 67

May God be gracious to me and bless me
May God make Her face to shine upon me. Please & Praise
Oh God, help me to remember Your grace and graciousness
That I might never forget that in You alone do I find salvation
Bring peace and unity, quiet and steadfast love
To my disordered internal world
That I might praise You wholeheartedly
Let me be glad and sing for joy with and for Your world
Let me remember Your fairness, Your grace
Let me trust You throughout my life. Please & Praise
Bring peace and unity, quiet and steadfast love
To my disordered internal world
That I might praise You wholeheartedly
You have blessed me even while I am troubled and doubting
You, You, God who is beyond my smallness, have blessed me
Welcoming me, even with my doubts and struggles, into
Your great cloud of witnesses
May You continue to bless me, undeserving though I be
Let me continue to revere You, praise You, thank You
All the days of my life, all the ways of my life. Amen

Psalm 68

Let God rise up and scatter my doubts and depression
Let all darkness and despair flee
Evaporate like mist in the sun
Melt like wax in the flame
Let my gladness, my happiness, my joy
Rise up with and to God
Let me sing praises to God
Let me lift up a song into the sky
Because God, my Lady Wisdom, gives me joy
Parent and protector
Provider and freedom fighter
No longer need I be a prisoner of despair
No longer need I live a dry, parched life
God, You lead people out of bondage
God, You keep people safe in the wilderness. Please & Praise
Powerful God, Wisdom God of desert and garden
You save me, time and time again,
Leading me back to faith, to belief, to joy
When You, God, are Ruler of my life
How I love it when my doubts and darkness flee
Disappear in Your power, Your grace
I feel rich, rich in the gold of Your power
The silver of Your grace
Scattering the thought-enemies
The feeling-enemies who attack my peace
What do mountains of earthly wealth and power count
Compared to the wealth and power of God's steadfast love
With might, untold unimaginable wisdom
God has conquered the worst of my inner enemies
Has led me to Her own place of refuge
God receives my praise and love
Even those parts of me that struggle
Blessed be the Sovereign God who daily bears me up
God is my salvation. Please and Praise
God is a God of salvation; to God, my Sovereign Lady Wisdom,
I owe my escape from doubt, despair, darkness, defeat
And death. Amen

Psalm 69

Save me, O God
From drowning in my own murky, dark thoughts and fears
I am sinking in that age old slough of despond, under the weight of sin
Sin without number, sin without name
Separating me from your life-saving buoyant steadfast love
Sin drowning me, attacking me, pushing me down, not even my sin
Just general despair at the sinfulness of this world
I feel its hate, I feel its despair, I feel its ugliness
I try to restore what I did not destroy, and I despair, I drown
God, oh God, You know my doubts, You know my conflicts
Am I going to worship You or reject You as myth
Am I going to honor You or forget about You
Am I going for the cynical or the hopeful; the worldly or the spiritual
Am I going to be scornful of my own puny faith
Sometimes I do not know my own mind, my own heart
I laugh at my own faith, doubt my own prayers
I second guess myself and You, O God
Like a drunkard, I wander without clear purpose
I shout and sing when I should quietly listen for You
I know, I know – I have to wait, to wait for Your right time
You will answer me, rescue me
In the abundance of Your steadfast love
You will lift me from the mire of my own doubts
Lift me above the deep waters of doubt
In which I flounder again and again
"Answer me, O God, for Your steadfast love is good; according to Your abundant mercy, turn to me. Do not hide Your face from Your servant, for I am in distress – make haste to answer me. Draw near to me, redeem me, set me free"
Free from my doubts, my second guessing
"I looked for pity, but there was none
For comforters, but I found none."
I poison my faith with doubts
My inability to be faithful leaves a sour taste in my mouth
It's up to You, God

You need to destroy these doubts, to keep me faithful
You need to redeem me, save me, help me, comfort me
You need to do it all
"I am lowly and in pain; let Your salvation, O God, protect me."
I will praise Your name, I will sing, I will give thanks
I long to be a shining example; I want to give hope to the hopeless
I want to have the kind of strong faith that inspires faith
But I am weak, God, and only You are strong
So save me, save us, please
Strengthen me, strengthen us, please
Build me up, build us up, please
So that we can live in Your steadfast love and salvation forever. Amen

Psalm 70

"Be pleased, O God, to deliver me." O Wisdom, "make haste to help me!"
End my doubts and confusion; grant me life and peace
Turn away my anger, my humiliation, my disquiet
Before it hurts me, before it destroys me
I envy those who are confident in You
Who rejoice always and are forever glad in their assurance
Of You and Your salvation
Who spend their lives, with no doubts, proclaiming Your greatness
"But I am poor and needy"
So if I am going to have any confidence, any peace
It will have to come from You. Could You hurry a bit, please?
I don't like to sound impatient, but I really need help
I need a deliverer
And that can only be You. So please don't delay. Amen

Psalm 71

You are not going to leave me to my worst tendencies
Now that I am old
Are You, God, my sweet Lady Wisdom?
I have nowhere else to go, no one else to turn to
No one else who can help, who can save me
Only in Your righteousness can I hope for delivery and rescue
Only if You hear my complaints, my need, my anger, my regrets
Only if You become the strong foundation of hope I can cling to
When the flood of negatives sweeps over me
Trying to drown me in despair
Only if You become the security of peace I can retreat to
Out of reach of the raging, crashing, hurting, killing negatives
The terrible Ds
Rescue me, O my God, from myself
Keep me from being unjust and cruel
Be my hope; be all that I trusted, all that I hoped for in my naïve youth
Just three weeks after I was born, I was baptized
Throughout my childhood, I learned of You
I was taught to praise You – and fear You – always
Oh how the nuns loved me then, but not so much later
Until much later – when I was long grown and utterly abandoned
I turned around – my own metanoia – and You were still there
You became, once again, my refuge from grief and hatred
I struggled, I was lost in disappointment, despair, despondency
Until I began to teach Sunday School
I didn't know what I believed when I started
I just knew that it felt good to be with children
And that, time and again, I found words, I found belief, I found joy
Beyond all expectations
And so You led me back and my days were filled with Your glory
Then Gordon died
And so much stopped for me
Struggle and doubt, depression and darkness
Marked my days again
But You didn't let me wallow
You sent the Johnsons and Mom and Norma
And others who needed me as I needed them

Now, again, my life has turned: You sent Woody
So now, although I still struggle, I believe You will not be far from me
You hasten to help me (though it doesn't always seem like hastening)
You deal with my doubt, depression, despair, darkness
You deal with all my death-dealing thoughts and feelings
So I will hope continually – in You
I will praise You yet more and more
I won't take credit myself but will give You credit
Because my righteousness is only borrowed from You
As You have saved the countless numbers, so You have saved me
And so I will praise Your mighty deeds for me, in me
I will praise Your righteousness, Yours alone
Let me remind You, if I may
That You ensured I learned of You in my youth
You were with me and led me to wonder at Your power and glory
Now that I am old, white-haired, I know that You will not forsake me
You will help me to continue to learn and teach of Your righteousness
From the depths of depression and doubt, You will bring me up again
You will comfort me, protect me, rescue me, save me, once again
And in return?
Well, I promise not to try to praise you with the harp or lyre
And although I will sing, it will not necessarily be sweet music
But I will remember, always, that it is You who rescues me
You and You alone who can keep me safe
You and You alone who defeats my own self-defeat
So I will keep writing, keep teaching,
Keep telling of Your righteous help. Amen

Psalm 72

In God alone – Creator Redeemer Sustainer Wisdom Woman God
Is there justice and righteousness; power to defeat my enemies
God alone can I trust to judge me with merciful righteousness
To have pity on my poor efforts
With God, my mountain-top gladness will be gladder still
With God, my oppressing valleys will be filled
My poor efforts will be blessed
I will be delivered from my worst troubles
And so may God be the sun and moon of my life, my eternity
May God bless my parched soul
With Her own sweet water of eternal life
So that through all my days
I may live in God's righteousness and peace
May God have dominion over all of my life: waking and sleeping
Highs and lows, triumphs and disappointments
Strengths and weaknesses
May my terrible Ds bow down before God
Because God can do what I cannot
God can ground my terribleness into dust
May I remember to give God the praise for my best
Let my worst –
Darkness, doubt, despair, doom-saying, depression, disgust, deceit –
Fall down before God
For God delivers me when I am needy and call, when I am down
When I feel alone
Without help or hope for redeeming my worst mistakes
God delivers me, redeems me, renews me, loves me even
God takes pity on me and saves my eternal life
From my oppressive faults, my violence to myself and others
God saves me, redeems me, renews me, loves me
Long may God live in me, in my mind and heart
Long may I give glory to God; long may I turn to God
In prayer and in thankfulness
May my life be turned around, yet again – one more time
And then again,

So that I turn from the dark to the light
So that my days may be filled with peace and blessings for others
So that I may enrich God's world
May God's name endure forever in my heart
May God's fame continue as long as I live under the sun
May I always – in all circumstances – bless God
Blessed be Lady Wisdom, the God of Sarah and Ruth, Esther and Mary
Who alone does wondrous things for me
Blessed be God's glorious name forever
May Her glory fill the whole of my life. Amen and Amen

Psalm 73

Truly God is good to me – and sometimes I even manage to act like
I deserve it – act like I am upright and pure in heart
But then, I stumble into doubt, slip into darkness
I stop valuing goodness and peace
And start desiring prosperity and power
I want power, success, wealth
I imagine that a better body, fewer problems
More self-confidence, more control is what I need to be happy
I fantasize about being better than others
Above mundane problems, above heaven and earth
I imagine the praise and adulation I would have from others
They would look to me; their envy would sustain me
My success would quiet my doubts
Otherwise what do I have?
What is the good of humility, godliness, innocence?
What has it gotten me? What good has come of all my efforts?
No good, no good at all.
I cannot quiet my demons, I cannot create my peace
Trying just wears me out
Only in Your house, only in Your grace
Only in Your wisdom do I find peace
Only in You do I find the true power that destroys all the false gods
That I worship, that I envy, that I think will be the answers I need
I wake to Your grace and my phantom gods disappear
And shrink to small ugly things
Here I can do no better than make the psalmist present:
When my soul is embittered, when my heart is pricked with envy
Then I am stupid and ignorant, no better than an unthinking beast
But even then, even when I forget Your **steadfast** love
Your power, Your grace
Even then I am always in Your **steadfast** love
Even then You hold onto me
Even then You wait for me to remember
You wait to welcome me back
Again and again

Whom have I in heaven but You?
What should I desire but Your peace?
All else fails, but You are the strength of my heart forever
Every mean and small part of me, all my terrible Ds, will perish
You will put an end to all my wrong-headedness, my false heartedness
You will keep me close, You will be my refuge
You will open my heart and my mouth
To tell of Your power and grace. Amen

Psalm 74

Here is the psalm of my distress; here is my nightmare
Where is my peace? Where is my God? Does God exist?
God's place in my heart, in my life, in my confidence
Is looking pretty damn desolate, destroyed, debased
Where is God's holy place in my interior castle
Where has that great cloud of witnesses gone
Oh the imagery of the psalm is the imagery of my soul
The imagery of my deepest, darkest fears
My life, my belief, my trust, my faith and my hope
Line by line, verse by verse, this psalm limns my despair
My peace is hacked to anguished restlessness
My faith is hammered to dust
My hope is smashed, shattered
My life is ashes
The worst in me out shouts the best
The darkness in me blinds the light
Why does bitterness not start with a D?
God, oh God, where are You? Are You real?
How am I to go on believing, hoping, trusting
The psalmist has me turn to God's creation
Seas and streams, night and day, crushed monsters
The psalmist may be impatient but never in doubt
Fearlessly, she calls to her God
Reminding her God of the power and the promise
Bold enough to command God
Do not forget the life of this poor person forever
So I turn to the psalmist
Though my world is dark and full of the violence of disbelief
And I borrow the courage of the psalmist to command God
Rise up in my mind, rise up in heart, rise up in my spirit
That I may rise again and praise You. Amen

Psalm 75

Thank You, God, for the times I feel You near
Thank You for the times I remember all You have done for me
Help me to remember that You will judge me
More fairly, more lovingly, than I judge myself
Help me to remember that it is in You that I find
Peace and security, though my world trembles
Please and Praise
Help me to remember that I cannot help myself
I cannot defeat my demon-enemies
The ones that are of my own making
The ones I carry inside
Not by insight, not by pills, not by counseling
Not by family, not by friends, not by accomplishments
Not even by prayer
Not I but You – You can put down the worst and lift up the best in me
You can poison all that poisons my peace
Then I will be able to rejoice forever
I will be able to sing Your praises, with that great cloud of witnesses
Help me to remember this
In You, all of my wickedness, all of my darkness will disappear
In You, because of You, my righteousness will shine. Amen

Psalm 76

On a beautiful, peaceful summer Sunday
All feels quiet and lush, both around me and inside me
It is easy to believe, today, in a great, benevolent God
A God who conquers my fears, my insecurities, my doubts
A God who defeats the "slings and arrows of outrageous fortune"
That constantly war against my peace, my wholeness
On days like today, it is so easy to praise a glorious God
A mighty God, who banishes my terrible Ds
So that none of them can harm me
It is easy to laugh at my doubts, depression, despair
Because today, on this beautiful day when my internal world
Seems simply a continuation of a beautiful natural world
Today, if I look no further than my home
If I think no further than myself
How easy it is to praise an awesome God
A God who defends me, who judges me kindly. Please and Praise
A God who stills my uneasiness
A God who lifts my oppressed spirit
Ah yes, today God seems awesome to me, in my life
God who conquers all
God who is worthy of my praise and my vows
God who is worthy of my gifts, my all
So easy, today, in the peaceful beauty of my home
So easy to echo the psalmist
But how do I keep this internal peace, this faith
When the world around me turns ugly
How do I understand an all powerful God
In the face of such injustice and ugliness
I do not know, so today I will enjoy a Sabbath rest
In the beauty of Your created world – a beauty that includes me. Amen

Psalm 77

"I cry aloud to God…that God may hear me"
I am troubled so I seek God, but not for peace but for rebuke
"My soul refuses to be comforted
I think of God and I moan"
I try to pray and I fail. Please and Praise
I try
Is it You, God, who keeps me restless and troubled
Is it You who keeps me focused on regrets and failures
Is it You would keeps me asking if You exist
And if You do exist, why do You seem not to care for me
Not to help me, not to let me feel, let me know
Your steadfast love, Your promised redemption, salvation
Your grace, Your mercy, Your compassion
Why do I feel oppressed by Your demands, Your displeasure
Please, Please, Please – I try to praise
I try to believe that it is me and not You who has failed
In belief, in love
Help me, please, to remember all the times You have rescued me
Help me to remember all the times of peace I have found in You
Help me to remember and believe Psalm 1
Help me to meditate on Your power, Your might
Your ability to conquer my demons
Help my mind to follow Your holy path, to rejoice in Your greatness
"You are the God who works wonders"
You are MY God, my God who has proven Your power in my life
Time and again
You have redeemed me, not once for all, but over and over again
Saving me from drowning in my doubts
Saving me from the torrents of my despair
Saving me from the arrows of depression, piercing my peace of mind
Overpowering the whirlwind of my feelings of defeat
Lighting up my darkness with Your enduring faithfulness
Your enduring faithfulness
That carried me through the raging seas of my doubts
So often I fail to see You, to recognize Your saving grace
Yet always You lead me, You gentle my spirit
You give me Your saints to guide and encourage me. Amen

Psalm 78

For seventy-two verses
The psalmist recounts God's **enduring** faithfulness
To the unfaithful
God gets angry, She punishes, She casts away
But returns again and again
Her **steadfast** love stronger than anger
Faithful to the unfaithful
Finding the lost, saving the good
Defeating the powerful, discarding the evil
With plagues, She freed Her people from slavery
Opened the closed sea for their safe passage
Closed the open sea against their pursuers
Through the desert She led them
With cloud and fire, miracles and commandments
Despite their doubts and complaints
She quenched their thirst, satisfied their hunger
In the promised land She established them
Preserved them despite their failings
Despite their desertion again and again
Through defeat, even in Her anger, She loved them
After the winnowing, with the remnant, for the good
She established Her sanctuary
Brought Her people back to Jerusalem
And always She gave them
Moses and Miriam, David and Naomi, Jesus and Mary Magdala
All Herself
Shepherding Her people with truth and skill
I am Her people
I am Israel's daughter
I follow until I wander
I believe until I doubt
I trust until I despair
I love until I become distracted, indifferent

I crave peace until I am hurt, angered
I am satisfied until I am envious
I laugh until I forget joy
I worship until I ignore my blessings
And still, always,
When I have flayed myself into pieces
When I am defeated, discouraged, depressed
When I have forgotten God
She remembers me
She rescues me, believes in me, loves me
She gathers the pieces of me
Saves the good, discards the rest
And brings me back to Her. Amen

Psalm 79

O God, I need help. My worst faults are defying my best efforts
Too often, I feel ruined, defiled, fit for nothing
I try, but I never seem to succeed for long
I feel scattered, drained, used up
Not really living but yet not dead
It feels like the more I try, the more defeated I become
How long, O God?
Won't You help?
You can do what I can't, but I do get tired of waiting
What am I waiting for?
Do I expect to wake up one day and be perfect?
All my struggles, all my trials, behind me?
Ah, that would be heaven.
Ha, yes, that would be heaven, only heaven
Never here on earth, never while I live here
But please, forget my failings and help me forget them
At least have compassion and help me have
Faith, Hope, Love
Help me, O God of my salvation,
For the glory of Your name
Deliver me and forgive my sins
For Your name's sake
Else I am surely defeated
Restore me, free me,
Give me faith in life everlasting
Scatter, at least for a while,
Those faults and failings that preoccupy me
That hold me prisoner, smothering my hope
Restore me, free me,
So that, knowing myself to be Yours,
I can spend my time praising You
Rather than fighting myself. Amen

Psalm 80

Renew my faith, oh Conqueror Wisdom Woman
Let Your light conquer my darkness
That I may see that I am saved
Hear me, see me, save me
You are Ruler, Leader, Guide, Savior for everyone
So stir Yourself for me
I know You have saved me – once for all
But knowing is not enough: I want to believe it
Renew my faith, oh Conqueror Wisdom Woman
Let Your light conquer my darkness
That I may see that I am saved
I'm crying here, do You see my tears?
Do You know my fear, my despair
I am so scared of the worst of me.
Renew my faith, oh Conqueror Wisdom Woman
Let Your light conquer my darkness
That I may see that I am saved
I am baptized, educated in my faith
Bible-reading, devotion-doing, psalm-writing
I pray, I do good works, I care about social justice
I go to church, I go to Bible Study, I read the saints
And still I despair. And still I fail. And still I struggle
Renew my faith, oh Conqueror Wisdom Woman
Let Your light conquer my darkness
That I may see that I am saved
I always expect more from You and from myself, don't I?
I look to You to defeat my enemies
Not believing that You already have
Like the psalmist, I bargain with You
Conquer my enemies, my fears, my problems
And I will never turn back from You
Give me life and I will call on Your name
How stupid, how foolish of me
To forget that You have already done it!
Renew my faith, oh Conqueror Wisdom Woman
Let Your light conquer my darkness
That I may see that I am saved. Amen

Psalm 81

I have reason to rejoice
To sing praises to God
To live joyfully
To celebrate
I have reason to rejoice
If only I can remember
That God has saved me
If only I remember to listen
For Her voice, Her reassurance
God relieves me, frees me
Answers me, rescues me
But also tests me and fusses at me
Wants me to listen and to obey
To obey – there's the problem
Sometimes I forget
Sometimes I can't figure out how
Sometimes I don't want to
Sometimes I lack the courage
Sometimes I don't believe
Sometimes I just ignore Her
I let it, let God, slip away
Until I once again feel overwhelmed
Lost, angry, sad, tired, defeated
Sometimes that's what it takes
For me to turn again to God
And let Her feed my hungry spirit
Fill my empty bitterness
With sweet faith. Amen

Psalm 82

My plea to God: How long do I have to go on knowing my failings
Living with doubt, depression, despair – my terrible Ds
Even while knowing myself to be blessed
Loving and being loved
Strengthen my weakness, O God,
With Your own strength
Restore my orphaned hope
Rescue my weak and needy spirit
Deliver me from my own wickedness
I have neither sufficient knowledge nor understanding
Time and again, I leave Your light and walk in darkness
I am shaken to my core
I reassure myself that I can make my own life good
But instead my efforts crumble into dust
So, please, God, rise up in my mind, my heart, my soul
That I may remember that I belong to You. Amen

Psalm 83

O God, do not remain silent
Do not turn a deaf ear, do not stand aloof, O God
I need You
Hear how Your enemies –enemies of my peace of mind – growl within me
See how Your foes – foes of my faith – rear their heads in my mind
I feel like my worst tendencies conspire against me
They plot against me even though You cherish me
"Come," they whisper to me, "we're stronger than your faith
When we're done, you won't remember God anymore"
With one mind – my mind – they plot together
They form an alliance against Your spirit in me –
Like Israel's enemies of old, these dark tendencies fight against my faith
To me they are indeed like Israel's enemies of old
And so I make bold to claim my inheritance as one of Your chosen people
Defend me as You defended Israel when its enemies said,
"Let us take possession of the pasturelands of God"
Make them like tumbleweed, my God, like chaff before the wind
So that they tumble from my mind, blow away from my life
As fire consumes the forest or a flame sets the mountains ablaze,
So pursue these enemies of my peace and faith with Your tempest
Terrify them with Your storm of righteousness and faithfulness, O God
Bury the unfaithful, doubting parts of me
So that I will ever seek Your name
May I never be ashamed and dismayed, may I never perish in disgrace
Remind me always that You, my God, Lady Wisdom
You alone are the Most High over all the earth – and over me. Amen

Psalm 84

How wonderful when my mind dwells with faith on You
Almighty, truly God
How often I yearn for that faith, envy those who have that faith
How often I ask why not me
For goodness sake, because of goodness, in goodness
Those whose lives are simpler than mine
Those who have the gift, the grace of firm faith
They are blessed with easy closeness to You
They live praising you effortlessly
They find strength – not confusion – in their faith
They go through life as through a beautiful valley
Watered by faith, swimming in pools of grace
Even in troubles, they go from strength to strength
Strength of faith, strength in God
While I flounder, drowning in pools of doubt
Hear my prayer – ah, but what is my prayer?
Do I really want You to make me a different me?
Do I really want the assurance of easy faith?
Do I really want to be an anointed one?
Here I am, God, believing – or trying to believe –
That better is one day in your courts than a thousand elsewhere
I read that You are a sun and shield, that You bestow favor and honor
That You withhold no good thing from those whose walk is blameless
But in my mind You remain elusive, You come and go
One day I may spend in the sureness of You, Your existence, Your grace
But a thousand upon a thousand I spend in darkness and doubt
Struggling against all that weighs me down
All the not good things and thoughts
God Almighty, what can I pray today except that You – You who may or may not exist – bless me as one who trusts in You and doubts You. Amen

Psalm 85
A prayer for the restoration of God's favor

My Sovereign Wisdom Woman, You saved me, You redeemed me
You pardon all my sins
Please and praise
Help me – again – Ruler of my life, to remember that
Help me to live it
Will I forever feel ignored by You?
Will I always lack confidence that You even exist?
Will I never believe what I hope to be true?
When will I simply rejoice in You?
In Your steadfast love despite my fickleness
Rejoice in the certain reality of my salvation
Speak peace to me
Help me be faithful and turn my heart to You
Let Your glory fill my life
Let Your steadfast love and enduring faithfulness
Seal my mind from doubt
Let Your merciful righteousness and sure peace
Kiss away my hurts, my angers
Let Your enduring faithfulness be my foundation
Your merciful righteousness my highest protection
Let Your goodness gentle me, guide me
Show me the way. Amen

Psalm 86
Supplication for Help against Enemies

Hear me and answer me, God, for I am poor in spirit and needy
Shall I bargain with You?
Preserve my peace of mind and I will be devoted to You
You will be my God
Well, You are God but I will worship You as MY God
Still, always, I come crying to You to save me
Although You already have
But I guess I am greedy as well as needy
Because I want more
I want You to save me from myself
I want You to make me happy, to lift my spirits
To prove how good and forgiving You are
To answer when I ask for Your help
To answer in the way that I want
[Shall I pause here to remind You how great You are?
That there is none other like You
That everyone and everything bows before You
You are great, You do wondrous things, You alone are God]
So here's what I want
First, I want You to teach me how to live as Your child
How to live in Your truth, how to glorify You always
How to revere You with an undivided heart
That's not too much to ask, is it?
After all, Your love for me is steadfast
You have already saved me
So, second, I want You to win my battles for me
You know my enemies: the terrible Ds
That destroy my peace, shred my faith, bury my hope
I count on You to be merciful and gracious
Please, I ask You, be slow to get angry with me
Be steadfast in Your abounding love for me
Be faithful to me even when I am doubting and faithless to You
Be gracious to me
Win my battles with Your strength
Save me, show me Your favor, help me, comfort me, heal me
Make me better, please. Amen

Psalm 87
A small psalm of quiet, enduring joy

I am created, founded, saved by God
My life is God's holy city and God loves me
In me, whatever my faults
Whatever my doubts, my darkness
In me is also, always, God's glory and grace
I focus so often on the darkness
Despair, depression, doubts, defeat
That I forget the victory
I forget that God Herself created me
Loves me, lives with me
I forget that God rejoices in me
Please and praise
When my heart sings
When my spirit dances
It is from You, God, that my joy flows. Amen

Psalm 88

Heman the Ezrahite speaks for me, cries out
All those thousands of years ago, as I so often cry out now
O Sovereign God of my salvation
When I end my day discouraged, crying to You
Hear me, let my prayer come before you
"For my soul is full of troubles"
I feel like hell
I feel like I am headed for hell
Do You forget anyone?
Have You forgotten me?
Have You cut me off?
Abandoned me to the hell of my own making
In the dark and deep regions of my mind?
Ah, I feel overwhelmed and I fear Your anger
Please help
I don't even like my own company
I want to rejoice and instead I cry
I want to feel thankful, not sorry for myself
I keep trying, really, God, I do
I try to come to You every day
But sometimes I think my soul is too deadened
And sometimes I think You are dead
Please help
Can I praise You from a dead heart?
Can I live for You if I feel like hell?
Now, this morning, once again, I come crying to You
Don't abandon me
(Even though sometimes I abandon You)
Don't give up on me, don't hide from me
See my desperation, my terror
As darkness closes in over me, as I drown
Hemmed in by my faults
My thoughts are in darkness, although it is dawn. Amen

Psalm 89

Now I will set aside doubt and darkness
And I will sing of Your steadfast love and enduring faithfulness
For a moment, I will let myself feel the eternity
Of Your steadfast love and enduring faithfulness
As if Your promise to be with me forever
Means I will never again feel doubt or darkness or despair
Because You can do that
Because You are greatest, most powerful
What is my darkness to Your light?
My doubt to Your enduring faithfulness?
You quiet my raging fears
You crush my threatening doubt
You scatter my confusion
You created me, all of me
The quiet and the tumult
The faith and the doubt
The confidence and the struggle
The light and the dark
You created all of me
To joyously praise Your name
You are strong, stronger than my best strength
You are steadfast love to my wavering
You are enduring faithfulness to my wandering
You are my happiness
In Your light, I shout for joy
I exalt Your name all day long
I live Your righteousness
For You are my strength, my shield
You are my sovereign
You promised me that I am Yours forever
With You, I am safe, secure
Chosen, anointed, strong
So I thought my doubts and darkness gone forever
I thought my world forever safe
In Your steadfast love and enduring faithfulness

Because You are my Parent, my God
And the strong foundation of my salvation
In You I have forever victory
In You I have forever peace
In Your steadfast love
You banish my doubts, my darkness
You discipline my heart and mind
You end my struggles
You remain true to me
In Your steadfast love and enduring faithfulness
Once and for all You saved me
Forever, for all eternity
And I thought that meant I would know only peace
Only Your peace that passes understanding
But the doubts return
Discouragement smothers my hope again
My doubts, my despair, my regrets
My sorrows, my failings
Once again plunder my peace
Where is Your steadfast love, Your enduring faithfulness
When I feel abandoned and defeated
Old and tired, trampled and cast aside
When I ask how long
How long, great God, must I keep struggling
How long the darkness
How long the doubt
Has my joy in You died forever?
Where is Your steadfast love, Your enduring faithfulness?
Remember me, great God, see me, hear me
I know that You have already rescued me
I know that
But sometimes I don't feel that, sometimes I can't live that
Sometimes I am reduced to a single hope
Blessed be God in my life forever. Amen and Amen

Psalm 90

God, You, You – I keep returning to You
Before I was, before anyone or anything was
You are
From everlasting to everlasting, You are God
In Your time, You will end my life
All my life and more is now to You
Compared to Your eternity, Your Is-ness
My life is grass, growing quickly
Withering just as quickly
I grew up fearing Your anger, Your wrath
Your hate of my sins
Your knowledge of all my secrets and my faults
The psalmist says our life is seventy years
Or perhaps eighty if we are strong
And those years will be spent "under Your wrath"
They will come to an end with a sigh
And in the meantime we will know only toil and trouble
I am seventy
Have I feared You enough?
What does that even mean?
How do I fear You and still know my sure salvation in You?
Where is my wise heart?
Did I understand Your steadfast love in the morning of my life?
Can I find joy now in Your enduring faithfulness for all my days?
With gladness I turn over to You the burden of my faults, my failures
With gladness I admit defeat and rely on Your glorious power
Let the favor of God, my God, be upon me
And quiet my tumult, preserve my peace
O please, quiet my tumult, preserve my peace. Amen

Psalm 91
Assurance of God's Protection

Living in the shelter of the Most High
Abiding in the shadow of the Almighty
I will say to Her
"You are my refuge and my strength
My God in whom I trust"
For She will deliver me from the snare of my doubts
And from my deadly depression
She will cover my faults with Her righteousness
Under Her wings I will find refuge and hope
Her enduring faithfulness is my shield against hopelessness
I will not fear my night terrors
Nor my daily failings
Not my dark depression
Nor my blinding doubts
A thousand doubts may trouble me
Ten thousand failings may preoccupy me
But She will protect me
She will open my mind to hope, to love, to eternal life
Because I have made Her my refuge
The Most High my dwelling place
No evil will befall me, no doom will come near me
She commands Her angels to protect me, to guard me always
To bear me up when I am cast down
To keep me from tearing myself to bits
So I will trample all my doubts and darkness, depression and disasters
God has promised
Through steadfast love, She will deliver me
With enduring faithfulness, She will protect me
When I call to Her, when I cry out, She will answer
She is with me through all my troubles, big and small
She rescues me, saves me, redeems me
With eternal life, she will quiet all my anxious striving
And show me Her salvation. Amen

Psalm 92
A song for the Sabbath

I will give thanks and sing praise to my Sovereign God, the Most High
I will remember and declare God's steadfast love in my youth
God's enduring faithfulness in my old age
With music and song, with prayer and reverence, I will give praise
My joy and my gladness are all God's work, God's great work in my life
Too great for my limited understanding
Though I struggle, though I doubt, though I fail again and again
God will prevail! I am saved, forever
Despite my struggles, despite my doubt, despite my failings
God succeeds, forever
And so I am saved and favored, a child of God, my Lady Wisdom
Destined for good, not evil
Destined for love, not hate
Destined for peace, not conflict
Destined for hope, not despair
Destined to flourish as God's good seed grows in me
And bears good fruit, even as I age
Maybe especially as I age
Because God is good, my gardener, my strong foundation
My savior, my righteousness, my Lady Wisdom. Amen

Psalm 93
The majesty of God's rule

The Almighty is sovereign, robed in majesty, stronger than death
She created me, all of me
And is with me always
In darkness and despair
No less than in light and joy
My emotions flood me
My wants drown out my peace
My fears thunder
My disappointments rage
But mightier than these is the Almighty, my God
Almighty God, Wisdom Woman, Your decrees are sure peace
Living with awareness of You is holiness forevermore. Amen

Psalm 93 - Again

God is sovereign, in majesty and strength
Creator of all, creator of me
And it is all good, secure forever and good
Except it is not
Evil exists
What we call sin exists
Separating us from good
Inside me and all around me
And I don't understand that
(But Paul says nothing can separate us from God's steadfast love)
Because God is mightier than evil, stronger than sin
Forever
Bigger, better, greater, more powerful
Than the floods of doubt, depression, despair, darkness
That roar high and overwhelm me
More powerful is my God, my Lady Wisdom
But still, still, those floods come
Overwhelming my good, my faith
Yet I am called to believe
Despite all evidence to the contrary
That God's commands are supreme
That God's own holiness is mine – Forever. Amen (and sigh)

Psalm 94

O Sovereign, You God of vengeance
You God of vengeance, shine forth!
Rise up, O Judge of everyone
Give to the proud what they deserve!
No, wait! I am proud, so often
With so little reason
Thank goodness, thank God
You do not give me what I deserve
But what Your steadfast love provides
But Sovereign God, how long shall I struggle
With the wicked, weak parts of me
With thoughts and feelings that I despise
How long will they trouble me
They crush me, Sovereign Lady Wisdom
They defeat my best efforts
I try to be good to all
Especially the marginalized, the disenfranchised
I try to be generous and merciful
But I forget, or I get tired or cynical
I am the dullest of people
Foolish when I should be wise
Forgetting Your knowledge of me
Forgetting Your teachings and Your discipline
You know my deep and lofty thoughts
Ha, You know they are but an empty breath
Bring me the happiness of Your discipline, O Sovereign
To order my unruly spirits
Save me, again, from days of troubled thoughts
Pits of dirty despair
Do not forsake me, do not forget me
Help me to live Your justice, Your righteousness
Help me to follow You with an upright heart
Who but You lifts my spirits
Who but You defeats my worst tendencies
If You do not help me, I am surely lost

Whenever I think that I will slip forever
Beneath my own muck
Your steadfast love, O Sovereign Lady Wisdom
Lifts me and holds me
When the cares of my heart are many
Your consolations cheer my soul
Can my best selfishness do that
Can I create a better world for myself
Too often I feel that my worst tendencies
My pride, my need to be right, my fears, my anxieties
My critical judgments of others
Too often I feel these band together to make me ugly
To destroy my innocence and joy
But You, only You, are my stronghold and refuge
In You my better qualities arise
With You my wickedness is defeated, wiped out
You, my Sovereign God, my Lady Wisdom, will wipe them out. Amen

Psalm 95

Let me sing a song of wonder and joy to Lady Wisdom
Let me rest in Her presence with thanksgiving
Let me make a joyful noise to Her with my song of praise
God is great
Sovereign over all the petty distractions of my life
Creator God, Maker of mountains and seas
Sovereign of the rich times and the parched times in my life
You created me
Blood and bones, skin and thought, sinew and feelings
You created me
So let me bow down and worship You
Let me kneel before You as my Creator, Savior, Helper
I am Yours
So, please, help me to live as Yours
With contentment not fear
Generous not grasping
Soften my hard heart
Do not despise me for my lack of faith
Because of my unruly heart's doubts
Lead me from my times of testing You
And quarrelling with myself about You
Please do not leave me stranded in my desert times
Thirsting without water
Doubting without faith
Demanding without gratitude
Wandering without rest. Amen

Psalm 96

Sing to God Lady Wisdom a new song
A song of blessedness, a song of salvation
A song of God's glory, marvelous works, and greatness
Sing to the God who is above all gods, above all troubles
Proclaim God's honor and majesty, glory and strength
God's holy splendor
I offer myself before my God
I offer myself and I tremble
God is Sovereign Lady Wisdom
And so God's world is firmly established
And shall never be moved
God's world around me
God's world inside me
God's living Word around me
God's living Word inside me
I live in God's world and God lives in me
God is fair and equitable
God is holiness and mercy
And so I shall be judged
With fairness, with mercy
Let me rejoice with all of God's creation
With seas and land
With field and trees
With thoughts and deeds
With feelings and senses
All sing for joy
Because God comes, God abides, God lives, God reigns
Judging all, judging me
With righteousness, with truth, with love. Amen

Psalm 97

There is one God, Sovereign and Almighty
I can relax, I can rejoice
There is one God, Sovereign and Almighty
One God who rules the universe and my life
With power and majesty, mystery and awe
With righteousness and justice
Burning away my doubts
Lighting my darkness
Melting my mountains of failure
From the heavens of hope
I proclaim God's righteousness
With clouds of witnesses
I behold God's glory
The glory of unfailing love
The glory of unending faithfulness
The glory that is stronger, brighter, surer
Than the false gods of despair that threaten me
I hear, I know, I laugh, I rejoice
For the certainty that You are greatest
Highest, bestest over all
Exalted far above the dark gods who trouble my peace
I rejoice for the certainty that You love me
You protect me, You rescue me
Light and lightness rise up in my heart
Joy and hope are born again in my soul
How can I help but sing?
Let me rejoice in God
And give thanks to God's holy name. Amen

Psalm 98

I sing to God a new song
I name God Lady Wisdom, Wisdom Woman and sing to Her a new song
I sing my own unique-to-right-now new song
And my new song sings of the eternal song
Of God's marvelous saving majestic powerful unfailing love
Of the times in my life when God's love is victorious
I sing because that is all times
I sing of the times when I know it to be true
I sing of God's steadfast love
God's enduring faithfulness
To me
All my life, all my life
When I know it and when I deny it
I live within God's victory for me
Make a joyful noise to God, O my soul
With that great cloud of witnesses
Sing and dance and shout for joy
Forget those terrible Ds
(At least for now)
Enjoy this sureness, this confidence
In the greatness, the triumph, the love of God
With all the waters of the seas
With all the depths of my feelings
With all the lands of earth
With all the breadth of my thoughts
With all the floods and mountains
With all my love and hope
I will sing my own ever-new song
Joining the everlasting song of joy
For the coming of God, Lady Wisdom
For the righteousness of God, Wisdom Woman
For the saving grace and equity of my God. Amen

Psalm 99

God reigns supreme over all my life
The good and the bad
The wanted and the unwanted
The then, the now, the will be
God is supreme over it all
I will praise Your great and awesome name
You are holy
I remind myself that You are
Not only the almighty Sovereign
But just and holy
With me as with Leah and Rachel
You rule with loving equity
Though I do not see or understand that truth
By faith alone
Let me praise and thank You
Do I dare join Miriam, Deborah and Hannah?
Do I dare call on You, depend on You?
Will You let me be Your people?
Though I fail so often
Though I love so little
Will You answer me?
Will You forgive me?
Is Your promise for me?
Am I a daughter of Israel?
Trying but failing
Needing forgiveness
As much as correction
All I can do is hope, believe
Exalt and worship You in my life. Amen

Psalm 100

With my whole heart and mind, body and soul
I will make a joyful noise to God
I will worship God with gladness
And come into God's presence with singing
I know that God is sovereign over all existence
Including my own
I know that God made me and I belong to God
I know that God claimed me for Her own
I, too, am a child in Her garden
So I enter God's palace home with thanksgiving
And Her beautiful courts with praise
I give thanks to God and bless Her name
For God is good, always
Her steadfast love endures forever
Despite my own fickleness
Her faithfulness extends through all seasons of my life
Through all my twists and turns
In times of doubt and times of faith
In times of devotion and times of dryness
God's faithfulness – TO ME – endures forever. Amen

Psalm 101

(This psalm is easy to focus internally)

Here is my forever prayer:
I will sing of loyalty and of justice
To You, God, I will sing
Of Your loyalty and justice to me
I will study the way that is blameless
When shall I attain it?
I will walk with integrity of heart
Throughout my life
I will not set before my eyes anything that is base
I hate the times that I fall away
I will not let doubt cling to me
I will know nothing of evil
I will recognize when my thoughts turn against others
And I will pray those thoughts away
I will recognize my own pride and arrogance
My haughty attitude
And will pray that pride away
I will value faithfulness to You
And to my better strivings
And I will nurture those within me
I will seek the company of those who try themselves
To live in loyalty and justice
I will not lie, I will not deceive
I will banish lies and deceit from my life
Morning by morning, day by day, night by night
I will pray that You destroy my wickedness
That You deliver me from evil
That You make Your home in my heart. Amen

Psalm 102

Hear my prayer, O my God, let my cry come to You
Don't leave me, I beg You, in distress and despair
Listen to me, hear me, see my need, my desperate need
You know my darkness
The days when my hope drifts away like smoke
When my faith burns away in fiery doubt
When my love shrivels like dry grass
When my hunger for You disappears into anorexic torpor
My spirit groans, even my body aches
With the pain of abandonment, desertion
I am reduced to a small creature of desert wastelands
My peace has taken flight
I lie sleepless and discontent
Wondering why I cannot be better than my worst parts
"My days are like an evening shadow
I wither away like grass"
Wondering why You cannot make me better
You could, You know, if You wanted to
Do I have to remind You that You are God Almighty
I capitalize Your name and even Your pronouns
To remind myself
You are God forever, almighty forever, my Savior forever
You do not forget me, You do not ignore me
Though many are the times when I find that hard to believe
I am of Your people; You are my God
You are victorious, glorious
You do hear me, see me, love me
Let me record it here and now: God loves me, saves me
God knows me, hears me, frees me
So I will praise and worship God and God alone
Some days, I feel as old as the earth that You created
As alone as the stars that You made
I will die, but You endure
I will die, but I live forever in and through Your love
You are steadfast in love, enduring in faithfulness, eternal
And so I will be secure, I will be established in Your presence
I will be holy as You are holy
In the meantime, hear me and help me, O my God. Amen

Psalm 103

Bless God, O my soul, and all that is in me
Bless God's holy name
Bless God and make sure to remember
All that God does for me
God forgives me
God heals me
God redeems me
God crowns me with Her own steadfast love and mercy
God satisfies me with good all my life
God renews me
(And yet, and yet, so often
I feel unworthy
I feel sick
I feel abandoned
I feel unloved
I feel old and worn out
I feel, even, that my faith is but a delusion)
I return to the psalmist who tells me that
God brings vindication and justice to the oppressed
God's people know God's ways and acts
God is merciful and gracious
God is slow to anger
God is abounding in steadfast love
And I can claim all, all for myself
This is why the psalmist blesses God's holy name
(This is what I sometimes do with my whole heart
And sometimes struggle to believe it even a little)
I go back again to the psalmist who tells me more
God will not accuse me
God will not be angry with me
God will not deal with me according to my worst
God will not exact vengeance for my doubts
God's steadfast love, love for me
Is higher than the heavens
God's forgetfulness and forgiveness of my worst

Encompasses my whole world
Separates me completely from my failings
(Really? Am I then still me?)
As a parent loves and knows the limits of a child
God loves me and knows my limits
(Though sometimes my fear is not fear of God
But fear that God does not exist)
Ah, but God knows, better than me
That I am but dust
(And you can't expect too much from dust)
My days are like grass
Once I bloomed strong and bright like a flower
But the wind of my days blows ever faster
My flower droops
The psalmist says, so what
You may fail, but the God's steadfast love
Is from everlasting to everlasting
God's righteousness is mine to claim
All the days of my life
While I try to keep God's covenant
And love as God commands me to love
God is sovereign over all
So with saints and angels
Let me bless God
Let me be among those who do God's bidding
Let me listen to – let me hear – God's Word
Let me join God's hosts, God's ministers, God's faithful
Let me join that great cloud of witnesses
Let me join the universe, God's creation
(Oh, please, with the humble peace that passes feeble understanding)
Bless God, O my soul. Amen

Psalm 104

The psalmist blesses God, Creator of the world
The psalmist worships God by naming God's creations
Extolling God's achievements
God is honor and majesty and bright light
God created everything
Heavens and light, clouds and wind
Fire and flame
The rocks of the earth
The deep waters of the seas
The edges and boundaries
Mountains and valleys
Water to quench thirst
Branches to shelter birds
Grass and food plants
Wine "to gladden the human heart"
Oil and bread
Trees, the psalmist's beloved cedars of Lebanon
The psalmist goes on and on
Reminding God of this incredible creation
Storks and goats and rabbits
The moon and the sun
Lions and their prey alike
How ecstatic is the psalmist
Verse after verse
Creation after creation
"In wisdom You have made them all"
Earth and sea
Creeping things and Leviathan
God gives and God takes away
Blessed be the name of God
God creates with God's own spirit
God takes away breath, and we die
And return to dust
"May the glory of God endure forever"
May God rejoice in Her works
In wisdom, in glory

Yes, but, my mind whispers
The God of the cedars of Lebanon
Is also the God of the plagues of Egypt
The God of wondrous creation
Is also the God of famine and flood
Disease and disaster
Pain and suffering
The Creator of everything
Is also the Creator of me
My generous intelligence and my unruly emotions
My comforting faith and my persistent doubts
My supple joints and my easy bleeding
My grand aspirations and my foolish distractions
My gracious loves and my unreasonable hates
My gains and my losses
My companions and my aloneness
My children's love and my children's withdrawal
My achievements and my disappointments
How I want to praise God as the psalmist does
Without reservation, with easy joy
How I want to accept
Life and death, good and bad
Giving and withholding, revealing and hidden
God, Creator, Redeemer, Sustainer, Lady Wisdom
The unknowable lover
The unreachable parent
The often forgotten ruler
How I want
To sing with the psalmist
To sing praise to God as long as I live
May my meditation be pleasing to You, my God
Let my sins, my doubts, my not-enoughs be consumed
Let my wickedness be no more
Let me shout with the psalmist
Bless God, O my soul
Praise God. Amen

Psalm 105

Let me start by giving thanks to God
By reminding myself of God's greatness and power
Power used for my benefit
Let me quietly, silently sing a song of praise
Praise for God's presence
In my life, in my heart
Let me glory in God, in naming God as my own
My own Creator, Redeemer, Sustainer
Lady Wisdom, as my own
Let my heart rejoice in God
I come back here again and again
Back to my psalms, back to my prayers
Seeking God's presence, needing God's strength
Reminding myself of God's power
Power to save me
Here and now, and at the hour of my death
And for eternity
Power for God's chosen people
Descendants of Abraham and Sarah
And I am one of them
Lady Wisdom, make me Your own
God is powerful and faithful
God is righteous and just
God of Sarah, Hagar and Abraham
God of Rebekah and Isaac
God of Leah and Rachel and Jacob
God of the great crowd of witnesses
Welcome me, please, among them
Choose me, pick me, protect me
Make me Your own
Keep my demons from defeating me
Keep my distractions from ruling me
Make me Your own
As You sent Joseph first into Egypt
Though as a slave
As You sent Esther to the king
Though she did not want to go

As You made Joseph strong and sure
Honored and safe
As You made Esther queen and savior
Make me Your own
Free me from the bondage of my will
Strengthen me to do the good I want to do
To help those who need help
Free me from own preoccupations
So that I can better do what is needed
Make me Your own
As Joseph fell and rose and served
As Israel came first to Egypt to be nourished
Then stayed as slaves
As Ruth came to Bethlehem a beggar
Then became a loved wife and mother
I rise and fall in my faith
I find success and pleasure and pride
Only to fall again into darkness, depression, despair and doubt
As You sent Moses and Aaron and Miriam
To rescue Your people in Egypt
Rescue me
Make me Your own
I know I rebel, I know I doubt, I know I despair
Help me to know that I am Yous
Not as one purchased with silver and gold, but as Your child
Guide me through my desert times
Feed my hunger, quench my thirst
With Your everlasting waters
Help me to remember Your promise
Your faithfulness, Your loving kindness
Make me Your own
Bring me into Your peace
Give me the only wealth I crave
The wealth of knowledge of You, sureness of You
That I might sing with joy
That I might live as You would have me live
That I might praise You
As You made the daughters and sons of Israel Your own
Make me Your own. Amen

Psalm 106
Nevertheless She Persisted

Praise God!
Give thanks to Lady Wisdom
For Her love persists forever
Can I ever thank God enough
Praise God enough
Wouldn't it be wonderful
If I lived my whole life
Praising God
Giving thanks
Acting justly
Doing what is right
Ah yes, then I would deserve reward
Then I would merit saving
Then I wouldn't need saving
But here's the sad truth
Time and time again
I forget
I wander
I grumble
I close my eyes to Her light
I stumble in my darkness, my blindness
When I feel enslaved by my own selfishness
I forget God is with me
When I wallow in my own doubts
I forget God drives those doubts aside
When I wander lost in the wilderness of despair
I forget God feeds my spirit
When I give my time, my worship to unwise pursuits
I forget the peace I find in God
When I sacrifice love to anger
I forget God's gentleness with me
When I live a half life, married to trivial things
I forget the fullness of life with God
When depression captures me

I forget God's power to free me
With the psalmist I look back
I look back on the long history
Of God's enduring love
To a faithless people
A doubting people
A grumbling people
A wicked people
A captive people
And I see myself
But I see God too
Her love
Her splendor
Her power
Her forgiveness
Her persistence
As always, for all people
She sees my distress
She hears my cry
She remembers me
She loves me
She saves me
She gathers me in
That I may give thanks to Her holy name
That I may glory in Her praise
Praise be to Lady Wisdom
Sovereign God of Israel
My God
From everlasting to everlasting
With that great cloud of witnesses
I joyously whisper shout, AMEN!

Psalm 107

Let me give thanks to God
For She is good; Her love endures forever
Let me remember and tell myself always
The story of my recurring redemption
How Lady Wisdom comes to me again and again
To defeat my dark tendencies
To bless my poor efforts
To gather my scattered thoughts
I wandered in my desert wasteland
Of darkness, despair, doubt and depression
I could not find my way to Her city of light
I was hungry for peace, thirsty for comfort
My hope faded
Lost, I cried out for rescue, for Lady Wisdom
And She came, with good news and the Way
She delivered me to the gates of Her city of light
Where my thoughts could settle
Where my darkness was banished
So I thank God for Her unfailing love
For Her wonderful help
For satisfying my hungry longings
For quenching my raging thirst
But then again I sat in darkness
In utter darkness
Prisoner in chains of my own making
I forgot God
I made my own plans, lived my own life
Went my own way
Until I stumbled, until I broke
Blindly, I cried out for rescue, for Lady Wisdom
And She came, with light and truth
She brought me out of darkness
Out of the utter darkness
She broke my chains
So I thank God for Her unfailing love

For Her wonderful help
For breaking the steel gates of my selfishness
For cutting the iron bars of my ignorance
But then again I became foolish
I left God
No dramatic rebellion but I left
Wandered away into other preoccupations
Into the tempting world
Until I felt like death, not even warmed over
Sickly, I cried out for rescue, for Lady Wisdom
And She came, with healing and life
She restored my faith, my hope
So I thank God for Her unfailing love
For Her wonderful help
For finding me
For curing me
With prayer and praise, with songs of joy
I give thanks
Yet again I was cast adrift
Scared and overwhelmed
Storms of doubt raged around me
Towering waves of despair crashed over me
I could find no lifeboat, no life preserver
Surely God's anger would weigh me down
Drowning, I cried out for rescue, for Lady Wisdom
And She came, with power and love
She stilled my storms of doubt to whispers of faith
She calmed my waves of despair
She guided me to Her safe haven
So I thank God for Her unfailing love
For Her wonderful help
I will join the great cloud of witnesses
In exalting and praising Her
I am God's creation
No less when my faith dries up

Than when it flows freely
I am God's creation
No less when my hope shrivels
Than when it bears fruit
I am God's creation
She turns my desert doubts into pools of faith
She turns my parched faith into flowing springs of hope
She shows me where to sow my hope
Where to plant my faith
With Her, I harvest the sweet fruit of love
She blesses me, and my comfort increases
My terrible Ds diminish in power
And yet, again, and again, and then again
I grow proud and am humbled
I grow careless and am brought to sorrow
I grow ugly and wander lost in anger
Until I know, again, how needy I am
How afflicted I am, on my own
Then She lifts me, again
Then She saves me, again
Then She reminds me again
That She is the Way, the Truth, the Life
She is Love
She is Lady Wisdom
She is Helper, Sustainer, Consoler
She is God
Let me be wise, please God
Let me remember
Let me ponder the loving deeds of God
For me – again and again. Amen

Psalm 108

The psalmist proclaims that her heart is steadfast
Ah, how I envy her
What is the opposite of steadfast
My heart is that – wobbly slow
Too slow, so often, to remember how good my life is with God
Too wobbly, always, to hold onto that truth
But this morning, this morning
Praise God
With the psalmist I sing and make music with all my soul
Quietly but surely the music of comfort plays around me
Hope dawns for me
If there is one consolation for being so often lost
It is this: the wonderful feeling, the dawn feeling
Of being found, of coming again from darkness into light
Of knowing myself to be part of that great cloud of witnesses
Of laughing with the new old knowledge
Of God's great love
God's highest, deepest, longest, surest faithfulness
So today I thankfully join the psalmist across eons
To pray
Be exalted, O God, above the heavens
Let Your glory be over all the earth
And, like the psalmist, I hastily add
Save me and help me, deliver me
Because You love me
I believe Your promises
Today I believe; always I want to believe
When I wander, when I despair, when I doubt
Is it not You, God, I wait for, hope for
Is it not You who has to lead me back to You
My own efforts are usually worthless
Until I turn to You, until I hide behind You
As You gain victory, again and again
Over my doubts, depression, despair, darkness
Ah yes, this morning they are defeated
I rest and arise this morning within Your victory
For me. Amen and Thank You

Psalm 109

Ah, God, wasn't it just yesterday
When I joyously proclaimed
Your victory in my life
Didn't I rest and arise within Your victory
And now, here I am
Feeling defeated
Here I am, about to rant
I am tired, God
I am tired of waiting for You to finally banish
My terrible foes
You know the ones, the ugly ones
The ones who scorn my prayers
How often have I named them for You
How often have they driven me from You
Doubt tells me You do not exist
Depression tells me I am worthless
Despair tells me this world is hopeless
Darkness tells me there is no light
Dis-ease tells me there is no quiet
Discouragement tells me to forget prayer
Distractions claim my attention
Bind them, burn them, banish them
Bury doubt in Your reality
Build Your mighty fortress to imprison depression
Bring hope to my hopelessness
Bank Your bright fires against my darkness
Be healing balm to my dis-ease
Blot out my discouragement
Bring my attention back to You
May this be how You, God, deal with my terrible Ds
That whisper and then shout evil
Poisoning my peace
Out of the goodness of Your love, Lady Wisdom
Deliver me
For I am poor and needy

And my heart is wounded within me
My hope, my joy fade away like evening shadows
I don't like myself, I don't like my choices
Help me, Lady Wisdom
Save me through Your unfailing love
Help me remember Your blessing
Help me believe Your power
Power to help me, power to save me
Your power with me always. Amen

Psalm 110

[...God chose to make known how great among the Gentiles are the riches of the glory of this mystery, which is Christ in you, the hope of glory...in whom are hidden all the treasures of wisdom and knowledge. Col 1:27 & 2:3]

God said to Jesus, "Sit at my right hand
Until I make your enemies your footstool."
God gave Jesus Her own power and authority
To rule over all, to defeat all foes
God has sworn to Jesus, "You are my high priest forever."
And – oh glory be! – St. Paul tells me Jesus the Christ is in ME
I can conquer my foes, those foes that destroy my peace
I can break and shatter, crumble and trample my terrible Ds
No, not me, but Christ in me
With the Holy Spirit of Christ in me
With Lady Wisdom's sustaining grace
I can lift my head from darkness and death
I can drink Christ's everlasting water
And thirst no more. Amen

Psalm 111

Praise God!
As Mary praised and magnified God
Who had done great things for her
So I give thanks and praise to God
With my whole heart I praise God
Who counts me among the upright
Among the congregation
Despite my failings
God's own work in my life is great
Delighting me and those who love me
God's work in my life is honor and majesty
Forever enduring righteousness
Despite my failings
I know God's wonderful deeds for me
I know God's grace and mercy to me
God nourishes my soul, sustains my peace
When I but remember Her
God remembers Her promises
God is faithful even when I am not
God shows me, time and time again, Her power
In my life, for me
God welcomes me as Her child, Her heir
I recognize God's work in me
As faithful and just, trustworthy and upright
God redeemed me; God loves me forever
Holy and awesome is God's name, God's power in my life
My reverence for God is, always, the beginning of wisdom
My forgetting of God is, time and time again, the forsaking of wisdom
May my life forever praise and honor God. Amen

Psalm 112

Praise God!
I am happiest, most peaceful, most content
When I live within awareness of God
When I delight in following Her way
The psalmist is right
The two ways of living contrast so completely
When God is a daily part of my life, my awareness
I move through my life with quiet assurance
I am thankful for my children and their children
I forgive easily
I feel blessed
I know myself to be rich in every way that counts
I trust God's righteousness in me, guiding my life
God's light can shine through me for others
God's light can shine through my own darkness and doubts
Because God is gracious, merciful and righteous to me
I can be kind and generous to others
I can work for justice
How I love those times when I feel secure in my faith
When I feel that I will never be moved from living with God
Then I am not afraid of troubles, of my own dark tendencies
My heart is firm, secure in God
My heart is steady, I am not afraid
I know that, with God, at the end of my life
She will give me triumph over my struggles
Meanwhile, I hope to live generously, wisely
Sharing what I have
Sharing God's righteousness all the days of my life
With God, through God, my own wickedness will melt away
My terrible Ds will not win
Out from my desolation, God will lead me to Her consolation. Amen

Psalm 113

Praise God!
Let me join the great cloud of witnesses
Who praise the name of God
Blessed in my life be the name of God
From this time on and forevermore
From my waking to my sleeping
May I praise God and what She does for me
God is highest, bestest, greatest
God is sovereign
In the world and in my life
My spirit is often troubled
My doubts return again and again
I struggle again and again with the familiar problems
Depression, doubt, despair, darkness, desolation
Rage and bitterness, jealousy and competition
They are real, they can be terrible
But God is greater
God is higher than my deepest depths are low
God is brighter than my darkest night is dark
God raises me from the dust of my troubles
God lifts me up from the ashes of my efforts
God clears my mind, my heart, my soul
So that I feel secure and honored, loved and protected
Just when I feel I have nothing left to give
Nothing worthwhile in me
God's fills my emptiness with Her grace, with Her joy
Praise God! Amen

Psalm 114

When God frees me from my slavery to discouragement
When Lady Wisdom blesses me with Her peace
My days become a devotion, my hope a sureness
My depression lifts
My doubts subside
My darkness brightens
I pray, I write, I love, I laugh
Whence these miracles
Is it magic or medicine
For me it is psalms, simply psalms
Not church, not theology, not deep contemplation
I will never understand it completely
But I observe it time and again in my life
My mountains of doubt fall
My drowning seas of rage retreat
My valleys of depression rise
When I welcome Lady Wisdom
When I turn to the God of Sarah
Of Hagar and Keturah
Of Rebecca, Leah and Rachel
Of Miriam, Deborah and Ruth,
Of Esther, Hannah and Jael
Of Elizabeth, Mary and Martha
Of Mary Magdala, Lydia and Priscilla
God who softens my hard heart
God who waters my parched soul. Amen

PSALM 115

Never mind congratulating myself
Getting all puffy and proud
All the credit belongs to God
Steadfast and faithful
Loving me even when I forget Her
God, my God, saves me
Why can't I simply rest in that belief
My soul wanders among other gods
I long to see accomplishments
To hear praise
To taste revenge
To curse those who hurt me
To smell wealth
To touch this world's best
I forget God, I doubt Her reality
I am blind, deaf, dumb
Senseless
Until I turn again to God
Until I believe and trust God
God who is my help and my protector
Until I trust the God of Sarah and Mary
God who is my help and my protector
Until I trust the God of generations
God who is my help and my protector
God remembers me, God will bless me
As she blessed Sarah and Mary
As She was with generations of believers
And doubters and even non-believers
Though I do not understand Her ways
Her whys and wherefores
Though I doubt Her wisdom and existence
Still I hope, hope that this is true
Because otherwise there is only silence and death
Otherwise I am lost
So I chose to believe and bless God
May it be so in my life forevermore. Amen

Psalm 116

I love God because She has heard my cries and pleas
Lady Wisdom never fails
I promise myself: I will turn to God as long as I live
Again and again, my deadly tendencies entrap me
Aain and again, my ugly enemies lay hold of me
I become distressed and discouraged, doubting and depressed
Again and again I have to call on God
"O God, I pray, save my life, my sanity, my faith!"
God is gracious – gracious and righteous and merciful
God protects the simple – and I am simple
God saves those who are brought low – and I am brought low
Return, O my soul, to rest in faith
For God will continue to help me, continue to save me
Continue to deal bountifully with me
You, God, and only You have delivered me from living death
Time and time again
From killing doubt, from deadly rage, from drowning depression
I cry but I also laugh, I stumble but I also skip, I doubt but I also believe
Help Thou my unbelief
Sometimes, when the darkness is on me, I think it is all a lie
I think You are a figment of imagination, of unfounded hope
But You never abandon me to those times
You rescue me, You restore me, You save me
Help me, God, to continue to honor You, praise You
Help me to remember Your reality, Your love, Your mercy
Help me to worship You
Precious in the sight of God
Is even the struggles, the trials of Her faithful ones
God, I am Your servant, the child of my mother
My mother, whose life has been spent in obedience to Your church
You loose my spirit's bonds
I praise and worship You
I offer You my life, which is already Yours
In Your great cloud of witnesses, I bow to You, I praise You. Amen

Psalm 117

Praise God, with everything I have
Exalt God, with everything I am
For great is Her steadfast love toward me
Her faithfulness to me endures all the days of my life
And beyond – endures forever
Praise God! Amen

Psalm 118

O give thanks to God, for She is good
Her steadfast love endures forever
When I am happy and content, let me say
Her steadfast love endures forever
When I struggle and doubt, let me say
Her steadfast love endures forever
When I am hurt and angry, let me say
Her steadfast love endures forever
In all circumstances, let me say
Her steadfast love endures forever
And let me rejoice
Distressed, I called to God
And She answered me – time and again
With God I do not need to fear
My own darkness, my own badness
God is on my side to help me
And so I shall triumph over my hates
I take refuge in God
God who is a safer shelter than all my own thoughts
Than all my own attempts
Than all my own philosophies and psychologies
My troubles, my failures surrounded me, overwhelmed me
Threatened to utterly defeat me
But God helped me, God saved me
God is my strength and my might, my salvation
And so I am quietly glad
Perhaps there will be other times of noisy gladness
Of shouting those glad songs of victory
But today, this morning, the quiet gladness is enough
To know that God is with me
Even when I fail to be what I want to be
To know that God is exalted
Even when I doubt that God even exists
I shall not die, I shall live
I shall live in God

I shall try to remember God's grace to me
I shall try to remember that God has saved me
I still struggle, I still feel abandoned at times
But God did not give me over to death – not ever
Let me enter into God's righteousness
(Having none of my own)
And give thanks
Thank You, God, that You have answered me
And have become my salvation
"The stone that the builders rejected
Has become the chief cornerstone."
The cornerstone of my life
This is God's doing and it is marvelous
This is the day that God has made
Let me rejoice and be glad in it
Again and again I have to come back to pleading
Save me, please, God, save me
Give me success in my struggles with myself
Blessed am I when God is with me
Blessed am I when I see by God's light
Blessed am I when I worship God
You are my God and I will give thanks to You
You are my God and I praise You
O my soul, give thanks to God
For She is good
Her steadfast love endures forever. Amen

Psalm 119

All happiness comes through knowing You, my God
Seeking you with my whole heart, walking with You
Oh, that I could be as steadfast to You as You are to me
Then joy and peace would come more readily
Then I should not sink in shame
Then I could praise You with an upright heart
Ah yes, then and then and mythical, magical then
It is not to be, but do not forsake me, O my God

By guarding my heart according to Your Word
By seeking You with my whole heart
By treasuring Your Word in my heart
I find freedom and peace, love and wisdom
Blessed are you, O God
Teach me where delight is truly found
Teach me to meditate on Your truth
Teach me to remember You

Can You please be generous with me so that I may live
Can you please open my eyes to Your wonders
Do not hide from me
I long to know You better
When I wander from You, I am unhappy
I start to feel only contempt and scorn
For myself and for others
Your enduring love is my delight and my best guide

Dust, my efforts are but dust unless You enrich them
When I pray, You listen (though I do not hear an answer)
Help me to believe, to understand, to remember You
I melt into sorrow unless You lighten my heart
I lose my way, unless You guide me
I choose to believe, I choose the God of the Bible
O God, let that be a good choice
Guide me, Lady Wisdom, enlarge my understanding

Eventually my life here must end; let me be full of faith throughout
Lady Wisdom, give me right understanding of Your Word and Your will
Let me delight in following You
Turn me from selfishness to generosity
Turn my eyes from vanities to life in You
Let me live within Your promise
Turn me from the disgrace, the terrible Ds that I dread
Look at me, I want to do good, I want to live within Your righteousness

Faithful to Your promise, save me, O God
Let me replace discouragement with trust in You
Let me speak truth, let me know hope
Let me live always within Your grace
Let my mind be freed from doubt and worry
Let me rejoice in my faith
Let me love Your righteousness, Your salvation
Let me love and honor You, let me meditate upon Your righteousness

Give me hope and peace in Your Word
"This is my comfort in my distress, that Your promise gives me life."
Keep me from arrogance
Let me turn to You, again and again, for comfort
I don't like myself when I forget You
I sing with joy and find my true home with You
Through my dark night, still I pray to You, O God
Let Your blessings fill my mind, my heart, my life

Help me, I implore You with all my heart
Remember Your promise to me that I may keep my promise to You
That I may always meditate on Your ways
That I may live as You would have me live
Even as I struggle within my own traps
Even in my own dark midnight, let me praise You
I want to be among Your great cloud of witnesses
Teach me to see Your steadfast love everywhere and always

I know You have been generous to me
Lady Wisdom, please bring me good judgment and knowledge
Help me when I wander; bring me back to You
You are good; You are God; You do good; teach me
Do not let my arrogance betray me
Do not let me become careless and complacent
Keep me humble, keep me coming back to You
Because You are better than any wealth or achievement

Just as You made me in Your image, give me Your grace
Let me hope always in Your Word and rejoice
Even when humbled, I am within Your righteousness
But please let me feel the comfort of Your steadfast love
Please show mercy to me or I will give up
Do not let my own arrogance subvert me from You
Let me be among those who turn to You always
Do not let me forget Your righteousness and goodness

Keep my hope in You, in my salvation, alive
You know how often I doubt and worry
I try to fill my life with You, but too often I fill it with empty vapors
How long will I have to fight those terrible Ds
I know it is my own arrogance that gets me in trouble
Your goodness endures, mine comes and goes, help me, please
I keep coming back to You although I wander often and get lost
Please, help me, save me, because of Your steadfast love

Lasting forever, Your Word is firmly fixed everywhere
Your faithfulness to me endures, and is my firm ground
I, with all of creation, am Yours
Without You, I would have sunk in my own misery long ago
You give me life and hope
You save me and make me Your own
On my own, my terrible Ds would destroy me
My best efforts accomplish little; in You alone is perfect help

Mediating on Your reality brings me joy and peace
In You I find truth and grace to overcome my failings
Knowing You is worth more than all my degrees
Years of life add nothing to wisdom and love without You
With You, with Your grace, I can avoid stumbling into evil
I want, I try to live within Your truth
Because within Your words, I find sweetness and strength
Within Your truth, I find comfort and understanding

Now Your Word is a lamp for my feet, a light for my path
Again and again I come back to You, to Your light
Again and again I fail: help me, please God
Hear my plea, fill my emptiness with Your grace
I try every day to live as You would have me live
Despite my failings, I do try
In You I find eternal truth and joy
I want to know and live Your truth forever

Oh, God, I hate my double-mindedness
With You and only You, with Your Word is safety
I pray for protection from my worst tendencies
Keep me close, that I may feel life and hope
Hold me close, that I may be safe and love You always
I wander away, into pride and reliance on myself
I trust knowledge rather than You, Lady Wisdom
And so I start to fear You rather than love You

Please do not abandon me to my oppression by depression
Do not let my doubts and disbelief oppress me
I get so tired of trying to feel saved, trying to believe Your promise
Forget my doubts and be generous in Your steadfast love for me
Grant me Your peace, understanding of Your righteous hope for me
You have to save me, God; You know on my own I fail again and again
Even though I try, even though I love being Your own
Even though I want to live always within Your Word and Your love

Quiet my doubts, O God, with Your wonderful truth
Lighten my darkness with Your Word and Your understanding
I wait, I wait with longing to live easily in Your truth
Treat me as if I love You, even when I doubt You
I depend upon You to keep me from my own failings
I depend upon You to help me live In Your truth and love
Make Your face to shine upon me, and give me Your peace
How sad it makes me to doubt, to forget You, to wander

Righteous are You, my God, merciful and just
Unlike me, You are always righteous and faithful
I try to love You but I defeat myself too often
I try to remember that Your promises, Your love
So often I feel small and despised
When I want to live within Your truth and everlasting righteousness
But trouble and anguish come upon me time and again
Please let me live in Your righteousness, Your love, Your wisdom forever

Save me, O God, help me to live well
Save me, O God, help me to live well
Morning and night, I need Your help, I need my hope in You
Morning and night, I need to pray, I need to seek You
Because of Your steadfast love, Your merciful justice, save me from myself
Thoughts, feelings that persecute me are too close to me, too far from You
And yet, You are always near, always true, even when I doubt and wander
Long ago, as a child, I learned of You, of Your foreverness, of Your reality

Take my misery into account and rescue me
Only in You can I have redemption and life
On my own, left to myself, I have no hope
So, please merciful God, give me life and hope
Time and again my doubts and troubles arise
Time and again I desert You
Please remember that I try, please keep me in Your steadfast love
Because You are eternal truth

Unwanted thoughts, ungenerous feelings attack me
So I run to You, to Your Word, for help and protection
I hate my own falseness; I love Your faithfulness
I come again and again here, to Your psalms
Here I find peace and sure footing
Here I find hope, here I find salvation, here I find You
Ah, I wish I had the psalmist's sureness, but I can only keep trying
Trying to follow You, to know You, to love You

Verse by verse, I cry to You, Lady Wisdom, for understanding
Please, please hear and answer me, save me
I want to sing Your praises as my rescuer and teacher
I want to sing Your praises as my promise and wisdom
Please, please say close and help me
I long for Your saving peace, I long to live within Your truth
I long to live praising You and depending only on You
When I wander, come find me, seek me out, return me to You. Amen

Psalm 120

In distress, I call out to God
Please hear me, answer me
Deliver me, O God
From lying to myself
From deceiving myself
From deceiving others
How is this to happen
How can I live truth and love
Ah, another D: deceit
How, God, how do I destroy deceit
I feel lost, without hope
A refugee exiled from God's kingdom
Too long have I struggled
Struggled with my own worst
Struggled with my own insufficient love
My own insufficient peace
I want peace, I long for peace
But too often I feel anger
So in distress, I call out to You, God
Please hear me, answer me
Deliver me, O God
Defeat my raging wars with myself
And grant me Your peace. Amen

Psalm 121

(Remembering Gordon)

Gordon thought the psalm meant that help was coming from the hills
I thought it meant that danger was coming from the hills
Gordon lived in assurance – he knew that God had him
Through the hills and valleys
Whether Gordon was faithful or faithless (be it to God or family)
When Gordon looked up, he always saw God, knew God's saving presence
For me, wherever I look, I see danger and doubt
Often, too often, darkness and despair
Help! Where is there help for my hopeless helplessness?
Ah yes, there is God – creator of heaven and earth
Surely, God is powerful enough to help me
God doesn't forget me, God doesn't desert me
God shelters me from my own despair
God shields me from my terrible defeats
God saves me from death
God keeps me from evil
God keeps my joy and my sorrow, my light and my darkness
My triumphs and my failures, my loves and my hates
God keeps ME – from this time on and forevermore. Amen

Psalm 122

Gladness fills my heart when I turn to You, my God
When I live within the comfort of Your Word
Not Your man-made images
Not the self-righteous religious
Not sermons or books
But within Your life within me
Within the sureness that Your goodness and mercy
Surround me, like a holy city
A holy city of love and justice
Ageless and eternal
A city with Your throne in my heart
Your throne of loving judgment
And wise choices
Within me as within each of Your children
Ah, God, my Savior and Wisdom
I pray that I may love You
I pray to live within Your peace and security
Let me reflect Your goodness and love for all
Let me work for Your peace for all. Amen

Psalm 123

To You I lift up my eyes
To You, enthroned in my heart, my history, my memory
As the eyes of a servant
Looks to her mistress
So my eyes look to You, my God
Until You have mercy on me
So, please, let it be so
Have mercy on me, O God
Have mercy on me
I have had more than enough of my own thoughts
My scorn for my failings
My pride for my successes
Have mercy on me, O God. Amen

Psalm 124

Let me remember it, feel it, say it
If it had not been for God who is on my side, always
If it had not been for God
My enemies, those treacherous thoughts and feelings
Would have swallowed me alive
My anger would have burned up my peace
My doubts would have drowned my faith
My distress would have washed away my joy
I would have drowned in the raging torrent
Of unruly emotions
Blessed be You, God
You, Who has not given me as prey
To the teeth of my own discontent
I have escaped, flown free like a bird
Like a young bird flying to the shelter
Of a mother's wing
Escaping my own traps and snares
My help is in the name of God
God Almighty, Who made heaven and earth. Amen

Psalm 125

May I please be, just for once, like Mount Zion
With faith unmovable, abiding in God forever
As the mountains surround Jerusalem
May God surround my life
From this time on and forevermore
God, please, keep me from wickedness
Keep me from doing wrong
Protect me from my terrible Ds
Be good to me, please, God
I try, I do try, though I fail so often
Do not leave me to my own crooked ways
Do not let my heart wander into evil
Rather, may Your peace be upon me always. Amen

Psalm 126

When God restored my peace
It was like a wonderful dream
I laughed; I shouted my joy
My friends said
God had been good to me
Yes indeed, God had been good to me
We rejoiced
Now, here I am, again, begging, again
Please, God, restore my peace – again
Let my sorrow, my distress be like tears
Tears that water the ground of my soul
Until Your grace and peace grow there again
Until I once again shout out my joy. Amen

Psalm 127

Here is what the psalmist reminds me:
Unless God builds my interior castle
I will never succeed in making it secure
Unless God guards the days of my life
I will struggle in vain to find joy
I can spend long days studying myself
I can fill myself with anxiety and worry
Useless and vain, all is vanity
I find rest only in God's love
These words, my prayers, are my heritage from God
The fruit of God's birthing in my life
Let my words, my prayers fly like arrows
Like arrows in Katniss' hands
Straight to God
These words, these prayers bring me such joy and peace
As they fly from me to God
In these prayers is my security, my safety
My defeat of my terrible Ds. Amen

Psalm 128

Joy, joy is mine when I walk with God
When I pray and write, when I pay attention to God
I am happy and it goes well with me
My life is like a vine, like an olive grove, like a garden
Bearing fruit, nourishing me and those I love
Blessing me, when I worship God
God, Mother Wisdom, who guides me
God, Father Creator, who blesses me
God, Brother Savior, who gives me hope
May I see You, worship You, believe in You
All the days of my life
Thank You that I have lived to see my children's children
God's peace be with me always. Amen

Psalm 129

Often have they attacked me from my youth
My terrible Ds: doubt, depression, discontent, discouragement
Often have they attacked me from my youth
Yet they have not prevailed against me
Thanks to God, they have not prevailed
They have scared me and scarred me
They have tried me and tied me
God, my righteous beautiful Lady Wisdom
God has cut those binding cords
God has turned back those enemies
In God, my fears wither
Until I forget, unless I forget
Unless I go my own way, believing God dead or mythical
Forgetting the reality, forgetting to pray
May the blessing of God be with me
I have victory only in the name of God. Amen

Psalm 130

Here I am again, God, crying to You,
Please listen, please help, please have mercy
I have failed again, of course
I smile outside while inside I am angry and disparaging
Disparaging: a new D in my firmament – my dark firmament of Ds
I know You forgive me quicker and more completely than I forgive myself
I know that is a fearfully, delightfully, wonderful thing
But does it help me? Will I be a better friend, mother, sister, daughter, lover
I wait for You, God, I wait and I hope
Right down to the bottom of my soul I wait, and I'll go on waiting
Through my dark night, through my dark night
Hoping, trusting, believing that the morning of Your light will come
With Your steadfast love, with Your full redemption
With Your saving grace
You will redeem me from all my sins, all my faults
I wait, I hope, I pray
I don't suppose You could hurry it up a bit, could You? Amen

Psalm 130 – again

Despite my dark doubts and confusion
Once again, I come crying to You, God
Hoping You exist, hoping You will hear me
Hoping You will help me
Because if You don't, who will, who can
I'm scared, I'm getting everything wrong again
I feel hopeless
Until I remember You, until I hope in You
Until I remember Your forgiveness
Your steadfast love, Your unfailing faithfulness
And so I have to wait, wait with hope for You
But it's so hard to just wait
Wait through this darkness
Wait through this doubt
Wait through this confusion
Wait for Your light to show me the way
The way, the truth, the life
Wait with hope, and belief in Your steadfast love
Your great power to help me, to save me
Because I am Israel's daughter and You are my God and Savior. Amen

Psalm 131
(My long-time favorite)

God of my hope, Savior and Spirit, Lady Wisdom
The times I love are the times when I am not preoccupied
With being smart, successful, happy, esteemed, accomplished
The times when I am not looking around to see how everyone else is doing
My heart does not stray outward
My mind does not chase round and round
Worrying about things I can't control, things I don't know
Things I'll never have, things I'll never understand
Those times, those times are my savasana times with You
My soul is calm and quiet
My contentment is deep
Deep as a child's quiet in the arms of a loving mother
You are my loving Mother
O please, let me – let me with that great cloud of witnesses
Hope in You from this time on forevermore. Amen

Psalm 132

God, remember me, take pity on my struggles
I swore – again and again – I swore to You, my God
To make my life Your dwelling place, Your temple
I swore to remember You day and night
Wherever I find myself
In all circumstances
I swore to keep You at the center of my life
To worship only You
Ah, but to do that, I need You to rise up
Rise up in my mind and heart
I need Your own righteousness
Not my failings
I need Your faithfulness
Not my fickleness
I need You to remember me
Before I can remember You
Please do not abandon me
I know Your promises
I know – or at least I was taught
That I too am part of the priesthood of believers
If I could but keep believing Your promises
If I could but keep obeying Your laws
Then I would deserve a throne with You forevermore
Ah, but that is impossible
Here is my only hope
Jesus once told His disciples
"What is impossible for humans, is possible for God"
So, please, God make me Your resting place
Sooth my troubled spirit so that You can reside with me
Bless me, satisfy me, save me
Cause me to shout with joy
Light my way
Defeat my doubts, my distress
Crown my life with Your peace. Amen

Psalm 133

How good and pleasant my life is
When my spirit is peaceful
When my belief is untroubled
Such times soothe my soul
Like soft oil soothes my skin
Sometimes, I feel that
Life feels easy
Sometimes, I feel that
"The quality of mercy is not strained
But falls as a gentle rain"
Sometimes, I feel that
God has blessed my life forevermore.
Thank God for those times. Amen

Psalm 134

Come, let me bless God
With that great cloud of witnesses
Let me make my life God's house
Let me lift up my hands in worship
And bless God
And, please, may God,
God almighty, God omnipotent
God creator of time and the universe
Please, may God bless me. Amen

Psalm 135

Praise God!
Praise the name of God
Give praise, O my soul, to our God
I am one of God's household
Not servant, but child
I enjoy God's favor
Praise God, for God is good to me
I will sing and shout for joy
For God is gracious to me
God has chosen me for Herself
I belong to God
I know that God is great
Greater than all my troubles
Greater than all my worries
Greater than all my doubts
God, mighty Creator
God, Sovereign in all the world, the universe
God of nature, God of humans
God of my world and God of my life
Let me remember what God has done in history
In the history of Her people
And in the history of my life
The times She freed Her people
The times She freed me
The times She defeated the enemies of Her people
The times She defeated my terrible doubts and distress
God's name, God's power endures forever
Through all the ages of my life
God helps me, saves me, redeems me
And has compassion on me
Power, riches, renown, even simple comfort
Are idols, the work of human hands
Unable to speak truth
Unable to see my needs

Unable to hear my pleas
Unable to give me life
If I trust such things to bring me happiness
I will find only disappointment
So let me live as one of God's household
Let me bless God
With that great cloud of witnesses
With Sarah and Miriam, Ruth and Deborah
Let me bless God
Let me honor the God of my heritage
Praise God! Amen

Psalm 136

O give thanks to God who is good
Whose steadfast love endures forever
O give thanks to God almighty
Whose steadfast love – for me! – endures forever
God alone does great wonders in my life
Because God's steadfast love endures forever
God who made me and all my world
Because God's steadfast love endures forever
God who gives me everlasting water
Because God's steadfast love endures forever
God who brings light to my darkness
Because God's steadfast love endures forever
God who guards my waking and sleeping
Because God's steadfast love endures forever
God who rescued and redeemed me
Because God's steadfast love endures forever
God who brings me through my troubled times
Because God's steadfast love endures forever
God who is with me even in my wilderness times
Because God's steadfast love endures forever
God who alone can remove my doubt
Because God's steadfast love endures forever
God who alone can lift my distress
Because God's steadfast love endures forever
God who alone can lighten my spirits
Because God's steadfast love endures forever
God who brings me Her wisdom
Because God's steadfast love endures forever
God sees my troubles
Because God's steadfast love endures forever
God rescues me from my troubles
Because God's steadfast love endures forever
God nourishes my soul
Because God's steadfast love endures forever
O give thanks to the God of my life
Because Her steadfast love – for me – endures forever Amen

Psalm 137

By the rivers of my distractions
I weep
I remember, long for, Your peace that passes understanding
But my joy is strangled in the branches of my despair
When I try to sing
My disquiet silences me
How can I sing of God's goodness
When I feel forsaken and exiled, depressed and distressed
And yet, when I forget God, when I doubt God
My spirit withers
My words dry up
When I do not set God
Above all other pleasures in my life
As my greatest joy and peace
Ah, God, I know these times of disquiet
When my heart tells me to doubt Your existence
Your power, love and grace
Ah, these devastating, depressing times
I will be happy when these times are banished forever
I will know Your peace when my terrible Ds are smashed
Smashed against the reality of You. Amen

Psalm 138

I give You thanks, O God, with my whole heart
Before all the demands of my life
I pause to sing Your praise
May that be true even when I feel too busy
Let me be grateful for my times and places of worship
Let me thank You for your steadfast love
For Your faithfulness
Let me remember
That Your name and Your Word are exalted
Above everything in my life
When I call on You, when I come crying to You
You answer me
You increase the strength, the peace of my soul
Through all the demands of my life
Let me praise you, O God, my Lady Wisdom
Let me pause to hear Your words for me
Let me sing – to myself – of Your mercy
Of Your great glory
For though You are Sovereign, almighty God
You help me, time and again
Only when I trust to my own goodness
Only when I become proud of my own knowledge
Do You seem far from me
Until I remember, again
That though I walk in the midst of trouble
You protect me and preserve my spirit
You deliver me from my troubles
You will fulfill Your purpose for me
Because Your steadfast love endures forever
Still, I cannot stop myself from pleading with You
Remember me, remember You created me
Remember me, remember You saved me
Do not forsake me. Amen

Psalm 139

O God, You know me, my work and my play
You know my best and my worst
My most secret and my most public
You know all my ways
You know my thoughts before I speak them, even to myself
You are here, with me, through my whole life
I don't understand it, I don't even always believe it
But there it is
I can't hide from You
Whether I am elated or depressed
Whether I am confident or dismayed
Whether I am filled with faith or doubt
Even when I decide You don't exist
You lead me, You love me, You hold me fast
Even when I am sure my life will be darkness forever
Even then, I am not darkness to You
I am still bright with Your love and faithfulness
It is just that I close my eyes to You
And then think that only darkness exists
But You have been with me from my very beginning
Because of You "I am fearfully and wonderfully made"
Because You are good and I am made in Your image
I cannot make sense of eternity
I cannot understand how You know my future
And yet I have free will
I could drive myself crazy trying to figure that one out
And in the end, I come back to the wonderful mystery of You
O that You would take care of my troubles once and for all, God
You redeemed me, You saved me, once and for all
Yet still I struggle, still I try – and fail – to be good, to do good
Go ahead, God, and search me
Root out all the parts of me that cause me pain, that disappoint You
Lead me in Your truth and love, in Your everlasting way. Amen

Psalm 140

Deliver me, O God, from my own evil
Protect me from my own violence
Keep me from unhealthy preoccupations
Keep me from anger and envy
Keep me from speaking ugliness and hurt
Please and thanks
Guard me O God, from my own wickedness
Protect me from my own violence to my spirit
The violence that traps me
In quicksand discouragement and doubt
Keep me from the trap of arrogance
Guide me away from the snares and nets
Of envy and anger, vengefulness and regret
Please and thanks
You are my God, my Lady Wisdom
So, please, hear me, answer me, deliver me
Stay inside my mind, stay in my thoughts
Do not give place to my ugly enemies
Please and thanks
Let my envy dissolve into gratitude
Let my anger burn away into compassion
Let my doubt be buried beneath faith
Let my words be generous and kind
Let my mind and heart, life and intentions
Be peaceful
I know You help the needy – and I am needy
I know You give justice for the poor
And I am poor in spirit and in faith
Lend me Your righteousness, Your wisdom
That I may give thanks to Your name
And live in Your presence. Amen

Psalm 141

O God, please hear me and help me
Let these prayers be my incense and sacrifice
Pleasing to You
Guard my thoughts and words
Guard my heart and actions
Give me patience and understanding
Give me generosity and wisdom
Do not let me turn from You
Do not let me become preoccupied
With my problems or my achievements
Let Your Word guide and correct me
Never let my own worst tendencies win
I pray, I pray, I pray always, please
Shatter my terrible Ds
Break apart my discouragement and doubt
Let me turn – metanoia – again and again to You
Be my refuge, my defense
Keep me from my own traps and snares
Ensnare my worst, that my best may escape
To live freely in and with You. Amen

Psalm 142

Here I am, again, God, crying to You for help
Complaining, reviewing all my troubles and failings
Because where else can I go but to You
On my own, I fall into my own traps, again and again
I cannot find the help I need
In any philosophies or psychologies
I cannot think or work my way out of distress
So I come to You, again, counting on You
Please help me for once again I feel trampled on
Brought low by my own failings
Those failings that are too strong for me
Those failings that imprison me
Without You, I have no hope
So please help me and I promise to be grateful
I hope to live within Your righteousness. Amen

Psalm 143

Would You please listen and answer me, God
I am trying to believe in Your faithfulness
That only in You is righteousness
I hope You are not judging me
Because right now I feel like I would not fare well
I'm tired, I'm sick and tired, and I'm angry
Here I am in darkness and doubt again
Feeling crushed, feeling pursued by my own failings
And feeling unheard
I have this appalling feeling that there is no one to hear me
I remember those times when I am sure of You
When I don't doubt Your reality
When I find peace and pleasure just in praying
In writing these psalms, in preparing Sunday School
In reading about You

But right now, all I feel is dried up and parched, again
I try to find You, but all I find is emptiness
Come on, God
I am tired of being polite
I am tired of being here again and again
I am tired of worrying again about Your existence
Tired of wondering if I am a fool
I can't find You, I can't hear You
I can't believe
In Your steadfast love
I want to trust You, trust
in You
But if You hide from me
How, how can I even
pray
For You to save me
When I can't even feel
Your existence
Come on, God, come on
Show up
If You are my God
Then be my God
Act like it
Show me how to be Yours
Lead me in Your goodness
Save me, save me, save me

Get rid of these troubling Thoughts and feelings
If Your love for me is steadfast
Then why won't You end my struggles
Why won't You let me live quietly
Quietly and surely as Your own. Amen

Psalm 144

Blessed be God, the bedrock of my peace
God who supports my best efforts
God who delivers me from my worst failings
God who alone gives my spirit refuge
And subdues my terrible Ds
O God, how can eternal You notice ephemeral me
Can You really care for me when I am just a dust mote
Taking shape briefly and then blown away
And yet, I dare to call upon Your help
Burn away my mountains of doubt
Pierce my darkness
Rescue me from drowning in my failings
Save me from my own deceits and pride
Then this dust mote will sing with Your grace
Though I have no talent, still I will hum and vibrate
With Your forgiveness, Your unfailing love
As You rescued David, as You were with Ruth
Claiming her for Your own
So You rescued and are with me
Save me from my own deceits and pride
May the thoughts that are born in my mind
Reflect Your truth and Your grace
May my actions towards others
Reflect Your love and Your support
Fill my life with Your goodness
Increase Your presence in my consciousness
Help me to share in creating Your peace
Do not let me wander far from You
Because only with You is my true happiness
Only with You is my assured peace. Amen

Psalm 145

I praise You, my Sovereign God, and bless Your name forever
Every day, every day, I want to bless You and praise You
I want to live within sureness of Your unsearchable greatness
I come back to these psalms to remind myself of You
To live again within Your majesty, Your wonder, Your mighty acts
So that I can proclaim again, to myself, the wonder of You
Of Your abundant goodness, Your enduring righteousness
You are gracious and merciful to me, slow to anger
Abounding in steadfast love
Good to me, to all of me, and compassionate because You made me
I want my life to be one of thanksgiving to You, O God
I want my life to speak, without words, of Your glory and power
Of Your love, Your splendor, Your salvation
I want to live always within Your truth, throughout my life
I want to believe in Your faithfulness, Your grace, Your reality
I need You to keep me from falling, from being bowed and broken
I need You to keep me close and to feed my spirit
I need You to open Your hand and give me what my spirit needs
I need to believe that
You are always just and kind
You are always near when I call
You hear me, answer me, save me
You watch over me, love me, protect me
I want to praise You, God, to give thanks for Lady Wisdom
Always. Amen

Psalm 146

Let me praise God
With every breath
As long as I live
Let me praise God all my life long
I want wisdom not more knowledge
I want sure help not false hope
I want healing not bandaids
All my knowledge, all my schemes
All my best efforts
Will die with me
My happiness, my help, my hope
Must be God
Immortal, almighty
Creator, Redeemer, Sustainer
Lady Wisdom
Faithful to me, She lifts my spirit
Loving me, She feeds my hope
God frees me
God's light banishes my darkness
God's steadfast love makes me whole
She comforts me, She protects me
She, only She, destroys my enemies, those terrible Ds
Let God reign in my heart forever
My God for all my life long
Praise God! Amen

Psalm 146 – Again

Alleluia! Praise God, Oh my soul
I will praise the Almighty all my life
I will sing to my God as long as I live
I will put no trust in perishable power
In plans that go nowhere
In schemes that offer no salvation
But I will count myself blessed
To rely only on my God
The Almighty God of Jacob, Leah and Rachel
Great God
Creator of all
Heaven, earth and sea
My heart, soul, mind and body
Guardian always of my truth
Lifting me from my oppression
Feeding my hunger for righteousness
Unbinding my spirit
Lighting my darkness
Straightening my crooked thinking
With steadfast love
Nourishing my weak yearnings for peace
Supporting my poor efforts at peace
So that God reigns forever
In my heart, my soul, my mind, my life
Through troubles and despite my doubts
As long as I live, my God reigns. Amen

Psalm 147

I will praise God – and feel good because it is right
God builds me up; God gathers in my wanderings
God heals my broken heart; God soothes my wounded spirit
The same God who created the universe
That great God almighty, powerful, all understanding
That God lifts up my downtrodden spirit
That God defeats my own wickedness
I hum, I vibrate with thanksgiving for God
God of growth, God of renewal, God of life
God of sustenance, God of soul food
God does not care if I am the best or greatest
God cares only for my hope in Her steadfast love
With God's great cloud of witnesses, I praise Her
For Her help, for Her strengthening of my weakness
For Her borning of my hope
For Her peace and Her bounty
For Her Word throughout my life, though I wander
She is God even of my darkness, my doubt
Even of the cold times of frost in my soul
Time and again She melts my frost
Time and again She blows away my doubt
Time and again Her waters of mercy wash me
And so I come, time and again, to Her
To be one of Her people, to live as Hers
Praise God. Amen

Psalm 148

Praise God! Praise God with my best and highest
Praise God with all Her angels and great cloud of witnesses
Praise God in my light and in my dark, in all my shining possibility
Praise God in my best times, my brightest thoughts
Praise God who created me
Praise God who keeps me forever and ever, secure in Her embrace
Even in the depths and monsters of my depression
Even in the frosts and fury of my doubts
From my high points and my low valleys
With my best gifts and my worst faults
With my wildness and my work
When I am flying high and when I am barely creeping
When I think I am ruling my own life
Now that I am old, as when I was young
Through it all, let me praise God
God of glory, God of wisdom, God above all
May God hold me close, may God keep me faithful. Amen

Psalm 149

Praise God! Can I yet find a new song of praise
Here at the end of my psalm journey
To be glad of my Creator
To rejoice in my Sovereign Lady Wisdom
To sing and dance, even if only inside myself,
For the sheer joy of living with God
God who is pleased with me, all of me
God who gives me victory over pride
Let me continue to try to be faithful
Let me continue, at least occasionally, to sing for joy
Let me praise God and rely on God
Let God be my two-edged sword
To sever my ties to those terrible Ds
Let God be my savior
To imprison my discouragement and doubt
Let God be my light
To banish my shadows of depression and deceit
Praise God! Amen

Psalm 150

Praise God! Creator, Savior, Spirit
Father, Mother, Brother
Wisdom, Teacher, Helper
Praise God in me
Praise God in Her universe
Praise God who has done wonderful things for me
Praise God because of Her surpassing greatness
Praise God with my singing words
Praise God with my dancing life
Praise God with my soothing faith
Praise God with my clanging doubts
Praise God with all the clashing, crashing reality of me
Because God made me, God saved me, God helps me
So let all of me, with that great cloud of witnesses
Praise God! Amen

BIBLIOGRAPHY

Alter, Robert. *The Book of Psalms: A Translation with Commentary*. W.W. Norton & Co., 2009.

Anderson, Bernhard W. *Out of the Depths: The Psalms Speak for Us Today*. The Westminster Press, 1983.

Bonhoeffer, Dietrich. *Psalms: The Pray Book of the Bible*. Augsberg Fortress, 1974.

Chittister, Joan. *Songs of the Heart: Reflections on the Psalms*. Twenty-third Publications, 2011.

Glazer, Miriyam. *Psalms of the Jewish Liturgy*. Aviv Press, 2013.

Glynn, Paul. *Psalms: Songs for the Way Home*. E.J. Dwyer, 1996.

Holladay, William L. *The Psalms through Three Thousand Years: Prayerbook of a Cloud of Witnesses*. Fortress Press, 1993.

Lewis, C.S. *Reflections on the Psalms*. Harcourt Brace & Co., 1958.

Lichtenstein, Aaron. *Book of Psalms in Plain English: A Contemporary Reading of Tehillim*. Urim Publications, 2014.

Merton, Thomas. *Praying the Psalms*. The Liturgical Press, 1956.

Miller, Patrick D. *Interpreting the Psalms*. Fortress Press, 1986.

Mitchell, Stephen. *A Book of Psalms*. Harper Perennial, 1993.

Paulist Press, *The Psalms: Singing Version*. 1966.

Peterson, Eugene H. *The Message: Psalms*. Navpress, 1994.

Prevost, Jean-Pierre. *A Short Dictionary of the Psalms*. The Liturgical Press, 1997.

Quillo, Ronald. *The Psalms: Prayers of Many Moods*. Paulist Press, 1999.

Wieder. Laurance (editor). *The Poets' Book of Psalms*. Oxford University Press, 1995.

Wilson, George M. (compiler). *Word of Wisdom: A Journey through Psalms and Proverbs*. Tyndale, 1996.

Bible Translations Used:

New International Version (e-book). Zondervan, 2011.

New Revised Standard Version Catholic Edition (e-book). Zondervan, 2011.

ABOUT THE AUTHOR

I was raised Catholic and attended Catholic schools through my second year in University, experiencing very conservative and very liberal teachings: pre-Vatican II Latin, ritual and Baltimore Catechism #3 in grade school; Vatican II and the social justice movement in high school; an introduction to Ignatian spirituality in university. However, I came to view organized religion as not just superfluous and superficial but also largely evil. Not until my 40s, when I accidentally discovered C.S. Lewis' *Mere Christianity* and *The Screwtape Letters*, and — one late night at a 7-11 store — an admittedly second rate novel (*Patience of a Saint*) by Andrew Greeley did I begin to acknowledge God's presence in my life and universe (or, in Greeley's terms, did God swing Her cosmic baseball bat and clobber me up the side of the head).

Now on Sunday I usually attend a simple Catholic Mass with my 94 year old mother in the sun-lit meeting room of a nearby "senior living community." I have worshipped and taught Sunday School in a Catholic church, an Episcopal church, a Missouri Synod and an ELCA church, but I won't join any church. My spirituality is greatly influenced by C.S. Lewis, John Stott, James Martin, Richard Rohr, Kathleen Norris, Anne Lamott, Joan Chittister and Elizabeth Johnson (to name a few), but also by Wangari Maathai, the Dalai Lama, Thich Nhat Hanh, my long practice of yoga, and a wonderful group of fearless Catholic women (#CatholicWomenSpeak). I definitely do not believe in the American version of inerrancy and sometimes I do not even believe in God, but I always find comfort and hope in the psalms.

My favorite things include writing, yoga, travel and just walking around outside with my husband, taking pictures. I took all of the pictures in this book, mostly with the camera in my Samsung cellphone.

As I write this description in November 2018, I am a soon-to-be-71 year old divorced, widowed and newly married retired academic living with my husband and my mother. I have some good, some fractured and some completely broken relationships with my far-flung children and step-children. I have thirteen grandchildren. I have incredible, life-renewing, faith-affirming friends. And I am deeply, wondrously, incredulously – miraculously, even – in love with my husband, Woody.

, one more thing: I have a name that, I think, is beautiful and serious-sounding, Adrienne Elizabeth. Alas, 'twas not to be. Since infancy I have been "Butsy" to all my family; since 1989 I have lived in Virginia. Hence my blog site name, vabutsy.

Made in the USA
Columbia, SC
12 December 2018